ROTARY CUT APPLIQUÉ
with Leaves Galore Templates

©2012

ISBN 978-0-9884279-1-4

Graphic Design and Printing by Palmer Printing Company
2902 South 3rd Street, Waite Park, Minnesota 56387

Published by
Sue Pelland Designs
4 Rockdale Hill Circle
Upton, MA 01568

suepellanddesigns.com

Introduction

When I started to quilt back in the 1980's, I was taught how to do beautiful needle turn appliqué. Quilters used to make appliqué templates out of cardboard cereal boxes. We would trace around this shape as many times as needed then cut with scissors. Squares, rectangles, and triangles were handled in the same way. Over the years, I have seen major improvements in cutting techniques for geometric shapes but there have not been many improvements in appliqué cutting techniques. I plan to change that!

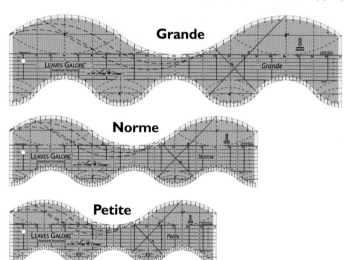

The Leaves Galore templates are a new way to cut appliqué. This book will explore the time saving techniques available to those who use the Leaves Galore templates. You could make all the quilts in this book with traditional appliqué methods but you will soon find that using Leaves Galore is so much faster and more fun. You will not want to make another appliqué quilt without them!

Why use Leaves Galore? Leaves Galore is the fastest and easiest method of cutting simple shapes for appliqué. The templates give die cut accuracy without investing in a die cut machine and dies for each shape. There is little fabric waste with my methods. We all know time is money and fabric is even more money! I will teach you how to save time and money by cutting with Leaves Galore.

While Leaves Galore templates can be used to cut fusible and hand appliqué shapes, they are designed with fusible appliqué in mind. There are no seam allowances built into the template measurements. A 3" curve on the template will quickly and easily make 3" leaves. If you use the templates for needle turn appliqué, your finished sizes are approximately ½" smaller than the cut size. Leaves Galore templates are great time savers for those who love hand appliqué. You can cut four layers of fabric at once. However, from this point forward I will only talk about fusible appliqué so we can assume that we are using the measurements on the templates.

The following chapters will introduce you to the basic shapes that will become your building blocks for fusible appliqué, including vines and four different leaf shapes. Next we will explore less conventional uses of the template such as making frames and creating your own wavy fabrics. One chapter is dedicated to teaching you how to make graceful serpentine and scalloped edges. Finally, several projects will give you the practice and confidence you need to create your own rotary cut appliqué quilts. You will never want to cut appliqué with scissors again!

So get your supplies ready, and let's have some fusible fun!

Table of Contents

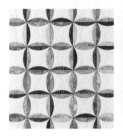

CHAPTER 1:
Fusible Appliqué Basics

Eve's Garden by Sue Pelland

FABULOUS FUSIBLES

Years ago, we wouldn't dream of making a bed quilt or show quilt with fusible appliqué. Fusible appliqué was known to be stiff and difficult to sew through. It was like quilting with cardboard instead of fabric. New generations of fusible products have changed my opinion of the quality of fusible appliqué and I now use soft, beautiful fusibles in quilts for my own use, for gifts, and for show.

FABRIC CHOICES

The greatest drawback of fusible appliqué has always been the stiffness of the fused pieces and the chance of fraying along the edges of the raw-edge fused patches. A very soft, new fusible minimizes the stiffness and produces a

soft, snuggly appliqué quilt. However, with such a light-weight bond, fraying on the edges can be a problem. Cutting fusible shapes with a rotary cutter instead of scissors reduces fraying on the edges of the cut patches.

You can use any type of quality cotton fabric for fusible appliqué but my favorite appliqué fabrics are batiks. Loosely woven cottons will fray more than tightly woven cottons. Batiks are typically made with a higher quality, more tightly woven base fabric making fraying less of an issue. I use batiks wherever I can especially for raw edge fusible appliqué.

When I am drawn to a fun printed cotton fabric for my quilt, I make sure it is a high quality printed cotton. Printed cloth is only colored on the surface of the fibers. When you cut the fibers there is a white core. With raw edge fusible appliqué, you might see that white core along the edges of the cut patch. Use a decorative stitch, such as the buttonhole or satin stitch around the edges of the appliqué to enclose the cut edge of the fabric. This will camouflage any white fibers showing along the appliqué edge.

TO PREWASH OR NOT TO PREWASH?

I prewash my fabrics. Period. Finishing chemicals on the surface of the fabric can interfere with the bond of your fusible. I also do not want to take the chance of my fabric colors running or seams puckering because of uneven shrinkage.

The recipient of your quilt may put your finished quilt through the washer and dryer so it is best to be sure your fabrics have already been machine washed and dried. Primarily, I do not want my fusible to misbehave. Your quilts will last a lifetime or more so take time now to prewash and you will never be sorry.

No fabric enters my sewing room without prewashing. As soon as I get back from the quilt shop, I trim the corners of the fabrics with scissors, separate by color (light and dark) and run two loads through the washing machine. If I have very small pieces or really deep rich colors that may run, I swish them in the sink with a dab of hand soap or dish soap. Rinse until you can see the water is clear. Next, I run all fabrics through the clothes dryer on a hot cycle, remove when damp, and press. I don't use any form of starch or sizing when pressing. Use only a spray bottle with water to get out all the wrinkles as this will ensure the best bond possible. Now I know that everything in my fabric stash is washed and pressed and I can jump right in and start cutting my next quilt.

WHICH FUSIBLE SHOULD I USE?

There are many fusible products on the market today. Your choice of fusible can make or break your finished quilt. My favorite fusible for appliqué is Mistyfuse. There are other soft products in quilt shops so do your research or experiment to find the one you like best.

You can use the fusible of your choice but I will explain the process for using Mistyfuse. If you use another fusible, just replace the word MISTYFUSE with FUSIBLE OF YOUR CHOICE. Make sure you follow the manufacturer's instructions precisely.

If you have not yet tried Mistyfuse it may look a little intimidating at first. Mistyfuse comes as a lightweight, fibrous web with no paper backing. You must use an appliqué pressing sheet or parchment paper to apply it to the back of your fabric. When using Leaves Galore, appliqué shapes are cut without marking, saving you time. There is no need to mark so there is no need for a paper backing. You will be cutting multiple layers at once and the paper backing makes those layers slip. If you choose a fusible other than Mistyfuse, remove the paper backing prior to cutting with Leaves Galore. With no paper backing to remove, the crisp, cut edges are maintained.

Avoid fusibles with a sticky side made to be repositionable. This type of fusible cannot be cut in multiple layers after removing the paper backing. The cut edges will stick together with the gummy temporary adhesive. If you do not remove the paper your fabrics will slip and you must remove the paper from each cut patch, definitely not worth wasting your time!

Mistyfuse is available online directly from Attached Inc., from suepellanddesigns.com or at your favorite quilt shop. It comes in white, black, and ultraviolet. It is available in 2.5, 10, and 100 yard lengths by 20" wide. I purchase white Mistyfuse in a 12" wide x 100 yard roll.

My ironing board is set up with a dowel that hangs underneath. Hang the Mistyfuse roll on the dowel so the fusible is always out of harms way when pressing. One hundred yards is a lot of fusible and a significant investment, however,

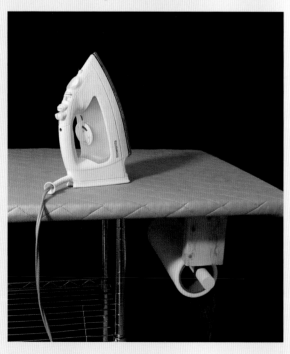

Mistyfuse has a long shelf life and it will not go bad before using it all. Cutting with the Leaves Galore templates is fast and fun and you will go through a lot of Mistyfuse. A Mistyfuse roll is a convenient way to purchase and store your fusible but only if you love it like I do!

APPLIQUÉ PRESSING SHEETS

Mistyfuse does not come with a paper backing so you must use an appliqué pressing sheet to protect your iron. You may already have one of these pressing sheets at home. It is sold as a craft sheet or a Teflon sheet and comes in white and brown. My favorite is the "Goddess Sheet" made by the Mistyfuse company. This brown Teflon and fiberglass sheet is extremely stable and durable and does not wrinkle, stretch, or warp. When using the Goddess Sheet there is a "Goddess Curve" on two corners. I keep the large curve on the bottom right hand corner so I know I am always pressing the same side. Both sides of the Goddess Sheet are the same but using the same side every time minimizes the chance of getting fusible on your iron.

Appliqué pressing sheets come in many sizes. The "Fat Goddess Sheet" measures 21" × 27". It is generously sized to fuse an entire fat quarter of fabric at one time.

You can also use parchment paper (not freezer paper) in place of the appliqué pressing sheet but there are two reasons I like the Goddess Sheet better. First, the pressing sheet is so shiny it transfers that finish onto the Mistyfuse. The Mistyfuse is so thin and sheer sometimes it is hard to tell which side the fusible is on, particularly when using batiks. If you use the appliqué pressing sheet, the shiny side of the fabric is the Mistyfuse side. Parchment paper will leave a dull finish on the fusible, making it hard to tell which side of your fabric is fused.

Secondly, the appliqué pressing sheet is better because you can see if there is Mistyfuse residue on it. Use your fingernails to scrape off any bits of fusible. Fusible residue on parchment paper is nearly impossible to see so you risk getting it on your iron or on the next piece of fabric.

If you do use parchment paper in place of the pressing sheet, pin or tape the parchment paper along one edge of your pressing surface so you are always pressing on the same side of the paper. Run your hand over the paper each time to ensure there is no fusible residue that will get on the pretty side of your fabrics.

IRONS
I use a very inexpensive dry iron from a discount store for fusible appliqué. It is easy to clean with Bohin Iron cleaner, and has no steam holes that will leave un-fused areas on my appliqué.

PRESSING SURFACE
My pressing surface is much larger than a standard ironing board. It is made from a sheet of plywood covered in two layers of thin cotton batting and a layer of cotton canvas. The board is attached to a metal shelf unit from a home center. This gives me a large, stable pressing surface that is not too soft and loads of storage below.

FUSING SUPPLIES
- Washed, dried, and pressed fabric
- Dry iron
- Fusible web of your choice, preferably Mistyfuse
- One or more appliqué pressing sheets
- Scissors
- Water in a spray bottle
- Large pressing surface

Applying Mistyfuse to Cotton Fabric: Step by Step

STEP 1: Set iron to cotton setting. Wash, dry, and press fabric. Steam as needed to remove wrinkles. Do not use starch or sizing.

STEP 2: Cut appliqué fabric to desired size for pattern and place right side down on pressing surface.

STEP 3: Lay fusible web over back side of fabric. Mistyfuse has no right or wrong side. Cut approximately ⅛" smaller than fabric to eliminate getting fusible on your ironing surface.

STEP 4: Lay appliqué pressing sheet over fusible. I sometimes use two appliqué pressing sheets, one on the bottom to protect my work surface and one on the top to protect my iron. As long as you cut your fusible slightly smaller than your fabric there is no need for the appliqué pressing sheet on the bottom.

STEP 5: Smooth iron over appliqué pressing sheet starting in the center and working toward edges, smoothing as you go to eliminate air pockets.

STEP 6: Wait 10 to 15 seconds for your pressing sheet to cool slightly.

STEP 7: Start peeling off pressing sheet from one corner. Watch as you peel it off to be sure no fusible fibers are sticking to the pressing sheet. All fibers should be melted onto surface of the fabric. If the fibers are stuck to the pressing sheet you have not heated the fusible long enough. Repeat the process to heat the fusible again until it is securely attached to the fabric.

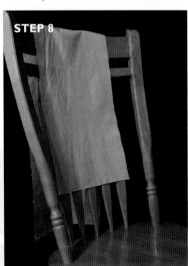

STEP 8: Lay the fabric over the back of a chair or lay flat with fusible side up. Do not fold fabrics or layer with fusible sides together until cooled for 15 minutes. After 15 minutes fusible is no longer tacky and will not stick to itself. It is safe to fold fabric for storage or to layer fabric for cutting.

CHAPTER 2:
Tools that make Rotary Cut Appliqué Fast and Fun

Springtime Ribbons by Sue Pelland, Quilted by Debbie Wendt

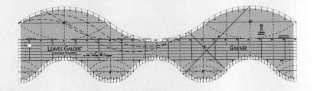

LEAVES GALORE TEMPLATES AS CUTTING TOOLS

The Leaves Galore (called LG for short) templates are ⅛" acrylic templates made for cutting appliqué shapes. LG templates come in three sizes which include Grande with an 8" and a 4" curve, Norme with a 6" and a 3" curve, and Petite with a 5" and a 2.5" curve.

Markings on the templates: There are many markings on the templates that you can ignore

completely until the time arises when you need them. Instructions in the following chapters will let you know when you need to identify and use each mark. A short description is provided.

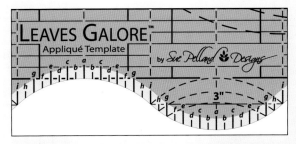

The size of the curve is measured from the inflection point of the curve, the point at which the curve changes from a concave to a convex curve. The inflection point is marked with a small letter "i" on every curve. From the inflection point "i", the small letters along the edge of the templates range from "a" to "i" and back to "a" again. Notice the curve from "i" to "i". The size of this curve is marked near the center of the curve with an 8, 6, 5, 4, 3, or 2.5" marking, depending on which template you are using.

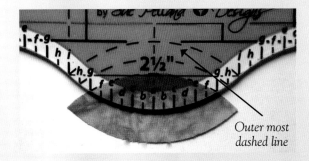

Outer most dashed line

There are several dashed lines along the edge of the smaller side of the template. The outermost line is the line used for cutting standard shaped leaves. You can make leaf sizes smaller than the standard leaf sizes of 8, 6, 5, 4, 3, and 2.5" by trimming your standard shaped leaves. Use the second and third dashed lines as a guide or use the small letters along the edge to trim the standard leaf shapes into smaller leaves. Note how we can use the edge markings to reproduce the same shape every time.

There is a long "Z" shaped curve line on the larger side of each template. This long "Z" shaped curve is only an indication of the shapes that can be made. When cutting "Z" curves, the letters along the edges of the template help you to keep the shapes consistent with every cut. See Chapter 4 for instructions on cutting the "Z" curves and the mirror image, or "S" curve.

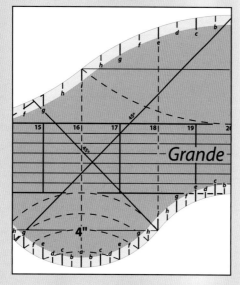

The diagonal lines help turn corners on your quilts. These lines are here for a reference point and you may require additional diagonal lines. You can use a template marking pencil (available in quilt shops or online) or a grease pencil to make additional markings on your templates. Cover your marks with cellophane tape to keep them from rubbing off. Remove the tape and marks when you are done using them.

The straight ruler markings in the center of the template help to keep your templates square to your fabric when cutting. These straight lines are also very helpful in turning corners or placing vines on borders. The square ends of the

template guide the quilter in keeping the template at a 90 degree angle for cutting and marking.

ROTARY CUTTERS

It is best to use a 28mm rotary cutter or smaller to cut with the LG templates. If you use a larger blade you will cut or nick the edge of your templates particularly on the inside curves. Even with years of practice using the tools for cutting I sometimes catch the edge of the template with my blade. If you damage your template you can easily sand out the damaged area with a piece of fine sand paper or an emery board. A foam emery board is part of my quilting tool kit just for this purpose. If you do not smooth out the damaged area, your blade will catch in that same spot each time you go past it when cutting. This can be frustrating! Take a moment to smooth away the sliver and your next cut will go smoothly.

It is imperative that you use a new sharp blade as often as needed. If your blade is dull it will push the fabric ahead of your cutter and create ripples along the edges of your cut curves. This is not noticeable when cutting straight lines. While your fabric is still getting pushed ahead it is eventually cut into a straight line. Can you see why it is a problem only with curves? Re-cutting edges to clean them up takes time and mis-cut leaves are a waste of fabric, so keep your blades sharp! The Grace True Cut Electric Rotary Blade Sharpener does a great job to give new life to an old blade.

Rotary cutters with a retractable safety shield and ergonomic style cutters are my least favorite tools. The retractable blade covers and ergonomic handles get in the way when cutting around curves. The stick style works best for cutting with Leaves Galore.

Many people like using an 18mm rotary cutter. These are wonderful around the curves and work great for cutting one to two layers, but I like to cut four layers at a time. However, if you do not mind cutting two layers at a time, use the 18mm for easier handling around curves.

The most common cutting problems my students have are caused by dull blades. A sharp blade will eliminate many technical problems like rough cut edges. Sometimes a blade is installed incorrectly. Refer to the rotary cutter instructions and make sure your blade is seated properly with all the parts in the right order. Two blades in your rotary cutter is another common problem that I notice in class. The blades often come two to a package stuck together with a bit of oil and it is easy to install two blades by mistake. Lastly, all blades are not interchangeable. Get the correct replacement blades for your brand of cutter. The center holes have different shapes. The wrong brand of blade may not turn correctly in your cutter.

Holding your rotary cutter: When using my rotary cutter, I hold it a little differently than most people. This helps me get better cuts around the curves. I place the butt of the rotary cutter handle in the palm of my hand, and wrap my ring and pinky finger around it to keep it there. This keeps the rotary cutter in line with my arm as if it were an extension of my arm. Holding it in this manner allows me to hold the blade at a right angle to my template and my mat. It also gives me more leverage as I can lean into the cut with my weight rather than pressing down with my wrist.

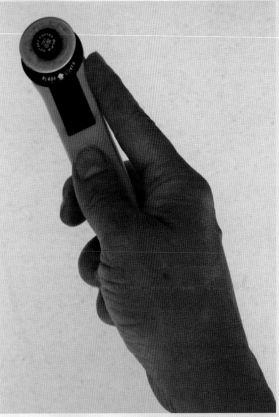

Notice the diagram on page 12. The blade angle is extremely important. Keep your blade upright and at a 90 degree angle with your mat. Do not lean the blade in or out but keep at a 90 degree angle with the template and the mat.

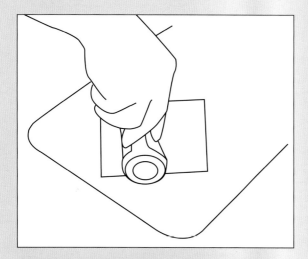

NO SLIP GRIPS

Slipping on fabrics can be a nuisance when cutting with Leaves Galore or any templates. I have found a wonderful product that virtually eliminates slipping. Grace True Grips are thin rubber disks that attach firmly to the back of your templates. Unlike sand paper dots that tend to fall off and leave a sticky residue, Grace True Grips will not fall off. You can remove them with no sticky residue, but why would you want to?

Three to four true grips are used down the center of each template. Do not place them too close

to the edges because you need to be able to push your edges down with tight contact to your fabric. If the grips are too close to the edge your fabric may move under the template as you cut. This will result in a ragged edge rather than a clean cut edge.

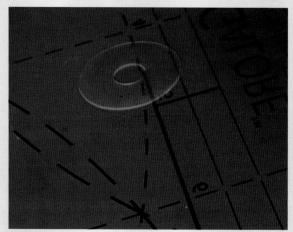

Grace True Grips come with fifteen grips to a package. One package will cover all three templates in my set with enough extra true grips for a ruler or two that you already have at home. They are a great value.

TROUBLESHOOTING WHEN CUTTING

If you get a rough edge:

🌿 Try cutting fewer layers. The maximum is five but try two or three to start.

🌿 Take your time, don't rush!

🌿 Make sure your fusible is down towards the mat. Sometimes cutting fusible side up makes the fusible stick to the blade.

🌿 Make sure you have grips on the under side of your template to eliminate shifting fabric.

🌿 Put a new blade in your rotary cutter or try a different handle if you have one.

🌿 Review the angle of your blade. It needs to be perpendicular to your mat and straight along the edge of your template.

🌿 Try a different cutting mat.

CUTTING MATS

Be sure you have a good cutting mat to use with your templates. If your cutting board is old and no longer pliable, you may need to replace it. After much use and over time, your board can lose its elasticity. Instead of your blade sinking into the board with every cut, your blade rides on top of your board and you may not get a clean cut. A new, soft, self-healing mat often solves the problem.

A few more tools that will make your life easier

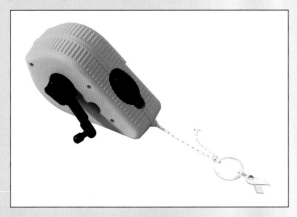

QUILTER'S CHALK LINE

Another tool I developed is the Quilter's Chalk Line. The Quilter's Chalk Line is based on a carpenter's chalk line and is used to make straight accurate chalk lines on quilts or fabrics.

The tool has a 30 foot cotton line inside a hollow plastic casing. The plastic casing has a door through which you can add powdered chalk. The line winds up inside the case and as you pull it out a thin layer of chalk coats the line. By stretching the line tight and giving it a snap, you can make a straight line between any two points. In my Chalk Line, I use iron-erasable chalk powder because I am often marking backgrounds for fusible appliqué. Fusing the appliqué with a hot iron removes the guidelines.

The Quilter's Chalk Line is the most efficient and accurate method of marking a grid for your appliqué backgrounds. The example on page 15,

"Melissa's Quilt," uses simple melon or leaf shapes placed on grid lines to give the appearance of a traditional Orange Peel quilt. This quilt is made not with curved piecing but with fusible appliqué. Many of my patterns feature quilts based on grids.

The Quilter's Chalk Line is a valuable tool when you need to square up your quilts prior to binding. You want four straight sides and four 90 degree corners on your quilts to help them hang or lay flat. By using your Quilter's Chalk Line and a large square template, you can easily mark four square straight sides on your quilts. If a mistake is made when marking your quilt, the chalk rubs or irons off so you can mark your edges perfectly before cutting. Marking with the chalk line prior to cutting eliminates errors in cutting. You will never cut off something important or cut crooked sides again!

One last way to use your Quilter's Chalk Line is for marking any straight line quilting designs such as cross hatching. There is no need to iron your quilt as the chalk rubs off with a microfiber cloth.

PATTERN CUTTING BOARD

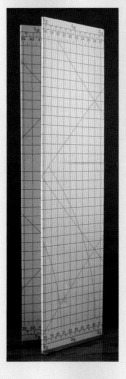

A pattern Cutting Board (left) makes marking grids even easier when used with the Quilter's Chalk Line. This cardboard mat is marked in one inch increments. Place your fabric over the printed grid so that you can see the markings on each edge. Use a T-pin to hold one end of your chalk line. Stretch the chalk line taut between parallel markings and snap. You will get nice straight lines on your fabric at exact increments.

ADDITIONAL MARKING PRODUCTS

BOHIN MECHANICAL CHALK MARKING PENCIL

This tool makes a very thin line that will not wear off before you want it to. The chalk colors can be changed but I keep this one for my favorite white chalk. I use this when marking hand or machine quilting designs on darker fabrics.

HERA MARKER

Used to mark along the edges of the templates. Held like a rotary cutter, this tool leaves a shiny line or crease as you press it into the fabric. I use this primarily for hand quilting designs marked with the template as the lines are a little more difficult to see when machine quilting. No removal is necessary and it works on all colors of fabric, even white.

CHALK WHEEL

There are a few different brands of chalk wheels such as the blue and red ones shown above. This tool is primarily used for marking quilting designs. I find it very helpful when marking placement of vines and serpentine edges as well. It can be used as is from the package, or you can throw away the chalk inside and replace it with iron-erasable chalk.

IRON-ERASABLE CHALK POWDER

This handy resealable bottle of chalk has a dispenser top to easily fill your chalk line and other chalk marking tools. The heat sensitive chalk evaporates when in contact with a hot iron (with or without steam). It also brushes away with a microfiber cloth.

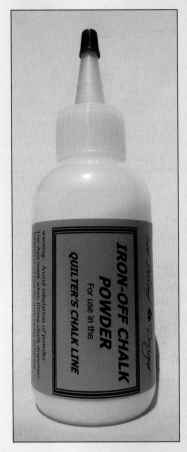

PILOT FRIXION PEN

Frixion is an iron away pen that comes in many different colors. I prefer to use chalk whenever I can, but on white quilts I use dots made with Frixion pens to mark the corners of my grids. Most of the time the appliqué will cover the dots, but if not, the markings go away with a hot iron.

Warning: The markings will come back if you put your quilt in the freezer (or store your quilts in a cold attic!)

CHAPTER 3:
Master the Cutting Technique

Melissa's Quilt by Sue Pelland, Quilted by Kathy Sperino

Diagram 1: 4" simple leaves drawn on paper shows how to nest leaves for the best use of fabric.

Four shapes become your "building blocks" for Appliqué

SHAPE 1A: SIMPLE/ STANDARD LEAF OR MELON

Simple/standard leaves or melons are the most common shapes in appliqué quilts. This is the perfect leaf or petal shape for so many appliqué projects. Entire quilts can be built around this one leaf shape as in "Melissa's Quilt" above. This quilt was made with 6" melons from the Norme template, the 2.5" leaf

from the Petite template, and the 8" vine from the Grande template.

The simple leaf shape can be made with any side of the three Leaves Galore templates giving you standard leaves in six different sizes. These six leaves can be trimmed to make even smaller leaves giving you a wide range of sizes for leaves or melons.

When cutting leaves in continuous lines, it is important to know how wide the leaves are, and the minimum width the fabric needs to be. Table 1 in the Appendix (p. 81) shows the size of the leaves, the size of the strips needed to cut these leaves, and the number of leaves in one strip. Also included is the number of leaves you can cut from a quarter yard of fabric.

Cut a Simple Leaf or Melon Shape: Step by Step

STEP 1: Place fabric fusible side down on cutting mat. Place your template along the right edge of your fabric. Use the straight edge of the template along the bottom edge of the fabric for the first cut. Make one serpentine cut.

STEP 2: Do not remove cut fabric to the right of your template.

STEP 3: Move your template up or down by one full leaf shape.

STEP 4: Line up the dashed line on the template with the cut that you just made.

STEP 5: Make a second serpentine cut. Now you can remove the cut leaves and the excess fabric to the right of your cuts.

STEP 6: Nest the next set of cuts right next to the first set off-setting the leaves by one half leaf shape as in Step 6 photo below.

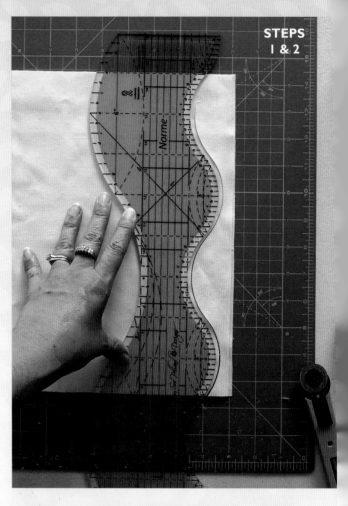

STEPS
1 & 2

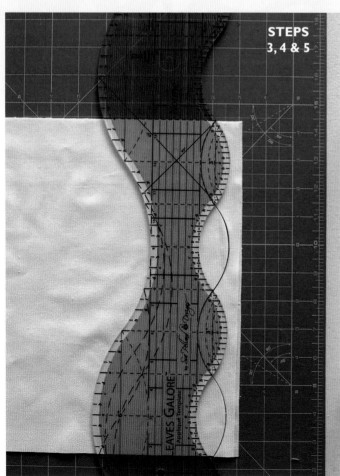

STEPS
3, 4 & 5

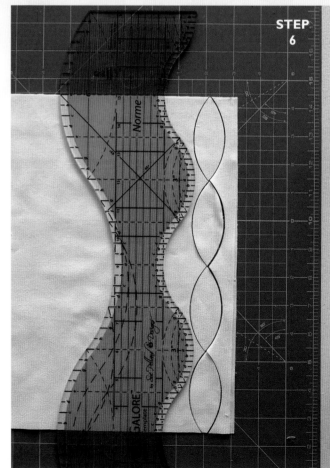

STEP
6

SHAPE 1B: TWO-TONED LEAVES

Two-toned leaves are simple leaves cut from a strip-pieced fabric. When sewing and pressing your strips, make sure you do not end up with "smiles" or strips that curve because of stretching during sewing or pressing. The best way to avoid "smiles" is to sew with an even feed or walking foot and alternate your starting points by starting each line of sewing at opposite ends of the panel. Once the panel is sewn, open your seams to minimize bulk. Iron fusible to the back of the entire panel keeping seams open.

Cut the strip-pieced fabric one layer at a time from the right side of the panel. You want the seam to go perfectly from point to point on your leaves, and it is difficult to do this while cutting more than one layer. Using the centering line that bisects the leaf shape on the template, place the centering line directly over the seam line.

Split Orange Peel by Susan Monsegur

up her two-toned leaves if she pieced her white background first. After piecing the background and pressing the seams open, lay the two-toned leaves over the background seams that make up your grid. There is no need to mark a grid on your background fabric!

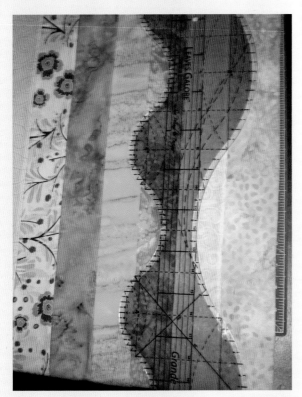

French Twist by Rana Heredia

Leaves can easily camouflage seams in your background fabrics when placed directly over the seams. Look at "French Twist" on the right by Rana Heredia. Rana decided it was easier to line

By combining your piecing and appliqué you have the opportunity to use multiple background fabrics.

SHAPE 2: "S" AND "Z" SHAPED CURVES

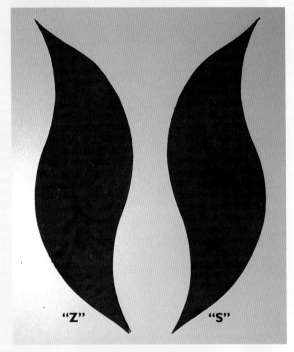

"Z"   "S"

"S" and "Z" shaped curves are exactly the same shape just mirror images of each other. They can be used for many different appliqué projects such as ribbons, ropes, and flowers.

The most useful "S" and "Z" shapes are cut with the small side of each template. The length of the "S" or "Z" shape is constant for each template size. A 3" curve gives you a 6" "S" or "Z" shape from point to point. Imagine the long graceful curve you get with the 8" side of the Grande template! This curve is 16" long so it is rare that I would use this shape in a traditional quilt. However the possibilities for contemporary or art quilts are endless.

The "S" and "Z" shapes can be cut in many widths depending on how far down you move the template with each cut. To keep the same width every time, you will be using the markings along the edge of the templates. These markings go up from "a" to "i" and back to "a" again. In this example we will use the letter "e" as it makes a nice width on the 2.5" and the 3" template. On the 4" template I like to use the letter "g" but it is a matter of personal preference and your desired result.

Look at Table 2 in the Appendix (p. 81) for detailed information on the size strips needed to make "S" curves, the size strips you need for one row of "S" curves, and how many curves you can get from a ¼ yard of fabric.

The "Z" shapes are cut in exactly the same manner but instead of your fusible side of the fabric being down on your cutting mat, turn the fabric over so the fusible side is on top. This will give you the mirror image of your "S" curve, a "Z" shaped curve.

Cut an "S" Shaped Curve: Step by Step

STEP 1: Place fabric fusible side down on cutting mat. Place your template along the right edge of your fabric. Make one serpentine cut.

STEP 2: Slide the template down and to the left. Watch as the cut edge and the template edge intersect. Look at the template edge and find the small letter "e". Adjust the template to make each curve end at the letter "e".

STEP 3: Make a second serpentine cut.

STEP 4: Now you can remove the cut leaves and the excess fabric to the right of your cuts.

STEP 5: Continue moving the template down and to the left to intersect at "e" for each cut. Note how the shapes nest and there is very little fabric waste?

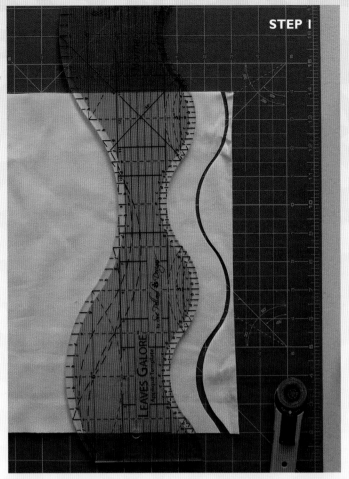

STEP 1

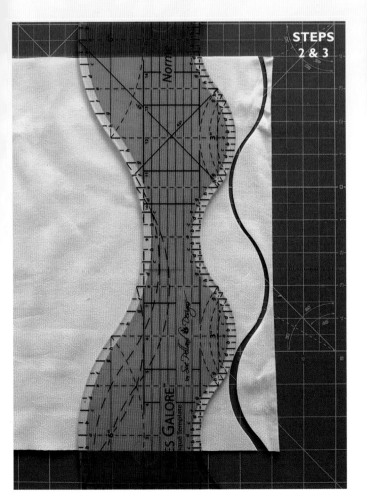

STEPS 2 & 3

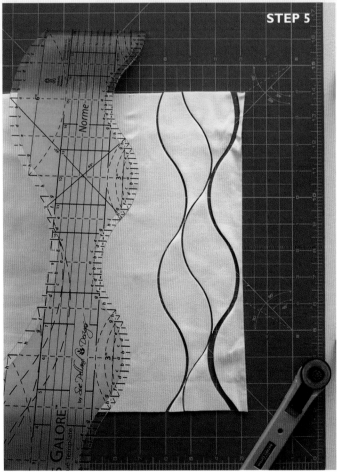

STEP 5

SHAPE 3: LEMON-SHAPED LEAF

Lemon-shaped leaves are the perfect leaf to go behind many different types of flowers such as daisies, poinsettia, and sunflowers. This shape also looks like a Christmas ornament. You can make a butterfly from lemon-shaped leaves. The "Magic Carpet Ride" quilt (p. 60) is made of lemon-shaped leaves cut with the 8" Grande Leaves Galore template.

Table 3 in the Appendix (p. 82) gives details for making lemon-shaped leaves including the size of strips needed, the number of leaves from a strip, and from a ½ yard of fabric.

Technically, the length of the lemon shape is two times the curve length. However, the points become so thin, they are only threads and do not hold together well. Trim approximately ¼" off

from each end to make a leaf ½" shorter than two times the curve length. This gives room to complete your decorative stitching on the points. You may choose not to cut the points if you are not using buttonhole or satin stitch to finish your edges. See Chapter 7 (p. 42), decorative stitching for stitching options.

As with the "S" and "Z" shaped curves, there is no waste when cutting your lemon-shaped leaves, except the partial leaves on either edge of the fabric. Of course, any leaf that is more than half a leaf can be tucked up behind your flowers.

Lemon leaves make great Christmas ornaments as in the example on the right.

Oh Christmas Tree, by Sharon Morris

Cut a Lemon Shape:
Step by Step

STEP 1: Place fabric fusible side down on cutting mat. Place your template along the right edge of your fabric. To maximize the number of leaves and to keep each cut parallel to the first, align the centering line marked with letter "a" on the bottom edge of the fabric. Make one serpentine cut.

STEP 2: Slide the template down and to the left by one full wave so the valley of one wave meets the peak of the other. Again, use the straight bottom edge to make sure you are one full wave down. Make a second serpentine cut.

STEP 3: Continue moving template up or down and to the left. Keep the same letter on the template lined up with the bottom edge of the fabric each time you cut (ideally letter "a"). The letter will be the same whether you are making your first or second cut.

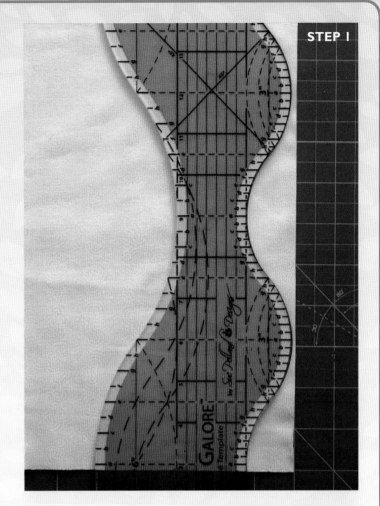

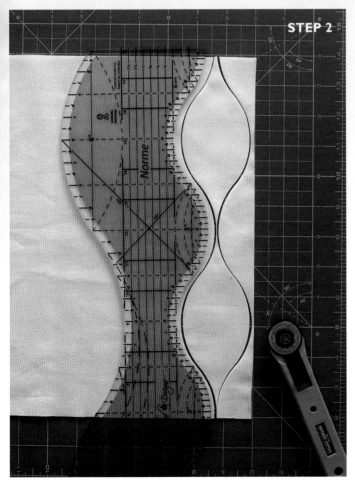

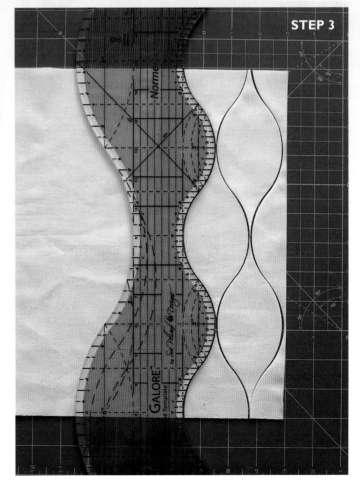

SHAPE 4: VINES

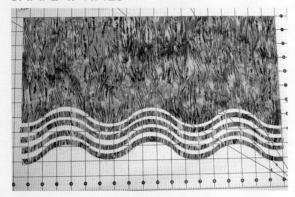

Vines make a beautiful finish to any quilt border and they can be used in row quilts such as the one on the book cover. Vine segments can be used to make appliqué album blocks as well as stems, branches, and Celtic style quilts.

Traditionally, vines are made with folded bias strips hand-stitched on both edges. Since we are primarily using the Leaves Galore templates for fusible appliqué it is easier and more fun to cut and fuse your vines.

One method of cutting is to use the length of your template as the minimum length of fabric for your vine. When cutting with the Norme template, I cut and prepare for fusing an 18" length of vine fabric. It is not necessary to cut a long vine as you can splice together two or more

lengths of vine and camouflage the splice by a well-placed leaf. To plan fabric yardage for vines see Table 4 in the Appendix (p. 82).

When making a continuous vine without splicing the vine, it is perfectly fine to cut from edge to edge on your fabric. However, you must be sure to keep the template lined up with your previous cut each time. Fold the fabric so you only have 22" to cut. Using the petite (15") or Norme (18") template, you will have to move the template once to cut from edge to edge.

If you require a longer vine segment, use a fused piece of fabric two times the length of your template. Fold the fabric and keep the fold toward you. Place the center line of an outside curve on the fold. On the smaller side of the template, you can use the straight bottom edge of the template. On the larger side of the template, you must use the centering line that bisects the outside curve. Place the centering line (ending at "a") on the fold. If you do not use the center line of an outside curve, you will end up with a point on the fold of your vine. This may be the perfect vine for your borders. If this is the look you desire, use the full leaf ending on the fold at "i" on your template. (See Step by Step on p. 23)

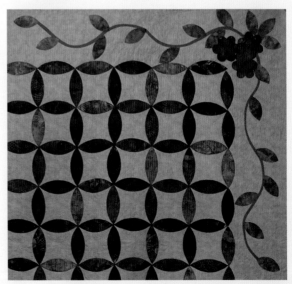

Strength & Hope, by Sharon Morris

22

Cutting Vines: Step by Step

STEP 1: Work with a piece of fabric the same length as the template, for two times the length, folded fusible sides together.

STEP 2: If cutting with the small side of the template, line the edge of the template up with the fold of the fabric. Cut one edge of the template from end to end on the edge of your fabric.

STEP 3: If working with the large side of the template, line the center line that bisects the leaf (marked with the letter "a") along the fold of the fabric.

STEP 4: Slide the template over by ¼" or more measured by a secondary template from the peaks of the mountains (½" in photo). You will need to measure the width of every cut vine to keep them consistent.

STEP 5: It is not necessary to cut a long vine. Splice the vines together and camouflage the splice by a well-placed leaf.

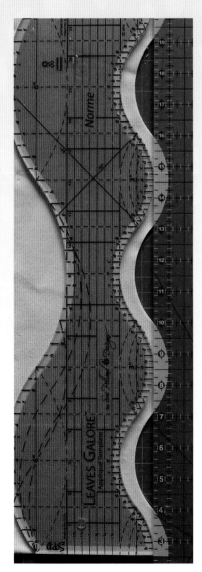

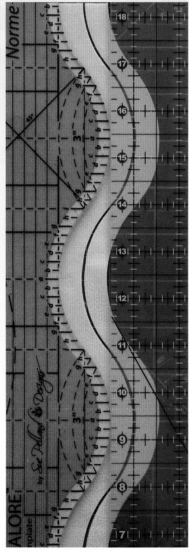

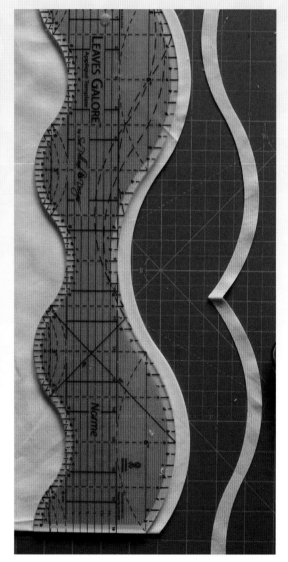

Keep straight edge of template along fold for a smooth vine with symmetrical curves.

Measure your vine width by using a long acrylic template alongside the Leaves Galore template.

If you don't use the center of the leaf "a" on the fold, you will end up with a point on the fold of your vine. This may be the perfect vine for borders. If this is the look you desire, use the full leaf ending on the fold at "i" on your template.

ADDITIONAL SHAPES TO EXPLORE

The basic shapes: Melon, "S", "Z", Lemon, and Vine are the building blocks for many appliqué projects. They are all made by a combination of two serpentine cuts with the two cuts running parallel to each other. These are the cuts that most effectively use your fabric and fusible.

There are numerous additional shapes you can make. Experiment with your templates and discover the possibilities. Try cutting standard shapes then altering them by changing the angle of the template, making a third cut, or combining two different size templates.

For example, I cut this 8" melon shape into two thinner 5½" long melon shapes used in "Joseph's Coat" (p. 54), or for the thin body of a butterfly (p. 32). The remaining center portion can be cut in two and used as the center of a flower. (Photo 1)

In Photo 2 on the left I used the scraps remaining from cutting with the 4" Grande template and re-cut with the 2½" Petite template to make a completely different leaf. Slide the template up or down to make the curve point in the opposite direction.

Feeding Frenzy (below) was made with random "S" and "Z" curves using the 3" template. Various widths were cut by sliding the template up or down and to the left of the first serpentine cut.

Cut pieces were arranged on a bright turquoise background to represent water and several of the green leafy waves were replaced with orange "fishy" "S" and "Z" curves.

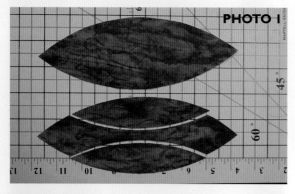

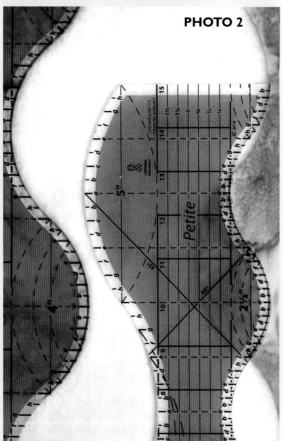

"Feeding Frenzy" by Sue Pelland

24

TRIMMING GEOMETRIC SHAPES

Geometric shapes such as squares, rectangles, triangles or diamonds make wonderful shapes when transformed with the templates. The "Hope's Diamond" pattern uses 60 degree diamonds trimmed with the Grande Leaves Galore template. Once the trimmed diamonds are arranged in a grid pattern on a whole cloth background they form leaf shapes between them.

Hope's Diamond by Sue Pelland, Quilted by Celine Spader

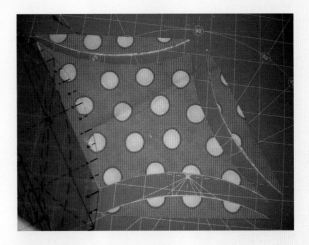

Boat sails in Joanne Bertrand's "Splish Splash" pattern began as rectangles.

CHAPTER 4:
What to do with your Five Basic Shapes, your Building Blocks for Appliqué

Orange Peel pattern. Generally, Orange Peel quilts are made with curved piecing. The same look can be achieved using fusible appliqué in a fraction of the time and with great accuracy.

A similar quilt, "Split Orange Peel," is in the Project Section of this book. Even though this quilt has a whole cloth background, it looks like it was intricately pieced with straight and curved seams.

"Mint Chocolate," also in the Project Section, has melons that are set on diagonal lines of pieced squares. Look at the Tips (p. 27) for combining piecing and appliqué. Choose the method that works best for your work style.

Melissa's Quilt (crib size) by Sue Pelland

THE STANDARD LEAF SHAPE AND TWO-TONED LEAVES: MELON QUILTS

My definition of a melon quilt is one using the standard leaf shape as a geometric shape not specifically as a leaf. To the right is an example of a melon quilt. This was my first pattern cut with the Leaves Galore template based on a traditional

TIPS FOR COMBINING PIECING AND APPLIQUÉ:

In quilts such as "Mint Chocolate" the melons do not cover the seam lines. Place the leaves diagonally on the blocks, complete decorative stitching, then piece the blocks together (Method One) or piece the background first and then add leaves (Method Two).

Method One: When your seams will not be covered with appliqué, it is often easier to complete appliqué and decorative stitching prior to piecing. This allows you to run your decorative stitches right off the edges of the patches without tying off your thread ends. Once piecing is complete, decorative thread ends are secured. "Mint Chocolate" is pieced this way.

Method Two: If you piece your background first your decorative stitching can be completed in long undulating curves. This is fun to sew and looks very nice. It can camouflage inaccurate piecing extremely well. The issue is that the larger quilt sections are harder to maneuver in your sewing machine. In the photo (p. 26), the borders on "Melissa's Quilt" had to be sewn on the quilt before adding the appliqué because the vines needed to flow over the seams.

With some quilts I combine both methods. Particularly with large quilts I like to appliqué a quilt in smaller sections, rather than forcing your entire quilt top through the machine to do your decorative stitching. Even a lap size quilt such as "Melissa's Quilt" was made in two sections. Manageable sections fit on my pin board to mark the grid and fuse the patches. It is easier to do decorative stitching on half the quilt at a time. Avoid placing appliqué shapes over the seam lines between sections. After making the sections, square up each with a ¼" seam allowance. Match sections with leaves tip to tip. Sew seams and press open. Fuse appliqué shapes over seams then finish decorative stitching.

TULIP

Tulips are made from one "S" and one "Z" shape as well as one standard leaf shape. Table 6 in the Appendix (p. 83) gives ideal size combinations for three different tulips. The tulip above is made from 2.5" "S" and "Z" shapes and a 4" standard leaf. The small leaves that frame the tulip are 2.5" standard leaf shapes.

Parrot Tulip: Use three or more "S" and two or more "Z" shapes to make a parrot tulip.

When cutting "S" and "Z" shapes for tulips, place fused fabric right sides together and cut "S" shape. This will give an equal number of "S" and "Z" shapes and they will be identical.

Use elongated "S" and "Z" shapes cut with the 5", 6" or 8" curve to form stems and leaves of tulips. Vary the widths slightly to give more natural looking stems and leaves.

POINSETTIA

Use small "S" and "Z" shapes cut using a 3" LG template then cut again with the curve to make two poinsettia petals from each "S" or "Z". Assemble flowers in three layers on appliqué pressing sheet, using the concentric circle diagram (Appendix, p. 97) beneath the pressing sheet.

Layer One: Make a dark ring of five to seven petals of both "S" and "Z" shapes. Keep points within the 7" circle. Press in place.

Layer Two: Make an inside ring of petals with the lighter color, slightly smaller than the outside ring, with light points between the dark points. Press in place.

Layer Three: Lift petals gently off pressing sheet and slide lemon-shaped leaves under petals. Trim leaves using ¼" overlap. Press back down and let cool. Remove flower and leaves from appliqué pressing sheet and apply to quilt top.

SUNFLOWER

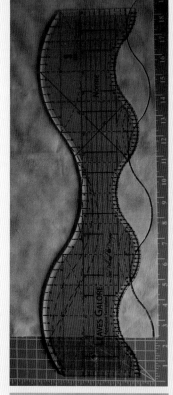

Sunflower petals are similar to "S" and "Z" shapes, however, to get them as fat as possible, it is best to overlap the template cuts so you end up with short fat petals. Make both "S" and "Z" shaped petals out of yellow fabrics. The 2½" template works best, but the 3" or 4" template can also be used, giving you a sunflower with a larger diameter. Cut a 2" to 4" circle from brown fabric for the center of the flower. Arrange petals around center circle on an appliqué pressing sheet, tucking ends under circle. Make lemon-shaped leaves with 2.5" or 3", or 4" template, the one which you used for the petals. Lift flower off pressing sheet and place leaves under as desired. Press lightly to adhere leaves to flower. Remove flower and leaves from appliqué pressing sheet and apply to quilt top.

WATER LILY

Water lilies such as these can be made with three "S" and three "Z" shaped curves together with four standard leaf shapes. I used the 2.5" curve on the Petite template to make the "S" and "Z" shaped curves and the 3" standard leaf shapes from the Norme template. The Mistyfuse is soft enough that multiple layers can be stacked on top of each other without creating an extremely stiff appliqué. Cut away excess fabric when possible to minimize bulk.

Layer One: Place one "S" and one "Z" shape together, overlapping, and offsetting tips as shown.

Layer Two: Choose another pair of "S" and "Z" shapes and add on each side of the center pair of petals. Repeat with a third layer of petals.

Layer Three: Choose four green leaves cut in a 3" standard leaf shape. Add first set of leaves horizontally about ¾" apart at centers.

Trim petals that fall below the center of this set of leaves.

Layer Four: Add a second set of leaves to cover over the trimmed petals. Press.

Layer Five: Peel completed flower off pressing sheet and place on quilt where desired. Press.

DAISY

Trace a 7" circle onto parchment paper or use the circle guide from the Appendix under your appliqué pressing sheet. Place four petals at N, S, E, and W markings. Press outside tips in place. Place four petals at NE, SE, NW, and SW markings. Press outside tips in place. Now arrange the center of the petals as you desire.

Pressing the outside tips first will keep the petals in place while you arrange the inside points. You can put the N, S, E, and W petals over the others or you can alternate the petals to form a radiating flower. Press in place as desired. Peel leaf edges from pressing sheet. Slide lemon-shaped leaves under flowers and trim away excess under flower. Press in place. Carefully peel away from pressing sheet.

BUDS OR MINI TULIPS

Flower buds are made with two standard leaf shapes in green and one standard leaf shape in the flower color. Mini tulips can be any color.

Buds: Place two green leaves at a 60 degree angle (or less) to each other, one slightly behind the other. Place a flower color leaf behind the two green leaves. This leaf can be even with the green leaves on the bottom or raised up as much as you like to make the color stand out.

Mini tulips are made the same way as buds with three flower colors rather than green leaves. Place the center petal over the right and left petals.

DRAGONFLY

Dragonflies are a beautiful design element that can enhance many appliqué quilts. Any wreath, basket, or bouquet of flowers can be improved by adding a hovering dragonfly.

To cut the elements for a Dragonfly:

• Prepare two different wing fabrics with fusible.
• Place two strips of each fabric fusible side down on cutting mat.
• Cut one standard leaf shape from this stack. If making more than one dragonfly, you can use the continuous cutting method to cut multiple standard leaf shapes from the stack of strips.
• Trim each stack of four leaves down to the second dashed line on your template to form narrow wings.

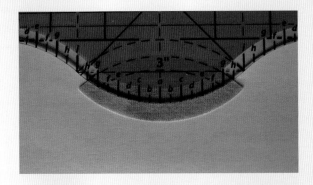

• Use one of the trimmed pieces to form the body and the narrow "leaves" for the wings.
• You may choose to cut a straight or tapered body using a straight edge template.

RIBBONS

Christmas Ribbons by Sue Pelland

Ribbons are made from "S" and "Z" shapes. Find the center of the border and mark a chalk line. Using all "S" shaped ribbon segments, alternate light and dark "S" shapes, overlapping ends by approximately ¾". Place one "S" shape with the tip and tail exactly on the center line. Tuck the tip of a light "S" under the dark "S" and lay the tail on the marked line. Keeping all the tails on the chalk line will ensure that your ribbon stays straight.

Use "Z" shapes to turn the top left and bottom right corners. All four corners can not be turned the same way. You can change ribbon direction by placing a flower or other appliqué motif at the corners where they do not turn gracefully.

Stitch ribbon edges with a satin stitch or close zig-zag stitch. Use thread that matches at least one of the two colors. You can also swap threads to stitch around each fabric.

ROPE

Splish Splash by Joanne Bertrand

Using either "S" or "Z" shapes, assemble rope between two marked lines on your quilt. When using the "S" shapes cut from the 2.5" template, mark two parallel lines 2" apart. For the 3" "S" shapes, mark two parallel lines 2.5" apart. Place the right and left side of each "S" curve just touching the marked lines. Place the next "S" shape right along the previous "S", tucking under the tips and tails, and butting the edges together.

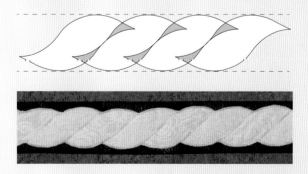

BUTTERFLIES

Butterflies are made from four lemon shapes made with the 3" template. This is a great way to use those lemon shapes that are not full lemons. Tuck two lemon shapes with missing points under two full lemon shapes. Add standard leaf shapes as desired to decorate the wings. Cut a long thin body by cutting a standard leaf shape (5" or 6") and re-cut as shown on page 24 into two thin leaf shapes. Thin strips cut with the 3" side of the template make the antennas. The 4" lemon shape also makes a nice full wing for a larger butterfly.

VINES

Cutting vines is covered in Chapter 3. (p. 22) Now that you have a cut fusible vine, the vine is

easy to stretch out of shape. Handle the vines with care to avoid stretching. To ensure that the vine remains the same shape it was cut, use the template to help lay the vine on the fabric.

Mark a straight line with your Quilter's Chalk Line where you want your vine to be centered or fold the border and finger press. Place the template on the fold with the center line of the curve on the fold or chalk line. Slide template over to the left by half the width of the vine. For example, if you have cut a half inch wide vine, center the

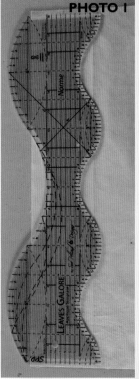
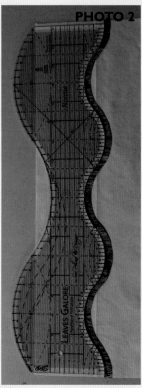

template on the chalk line, then slide to the left by ¼". Just estimate half the size of any vine and adjust by eye. It will not show if you are a little off as long as you make an attempt to center the vine.

Vines can be spliced so you do not need to have a long continuous strip. To splice your vine, place another vine segment after the first, overlapping as much as needed to match the curves. With sharp embroidery scissors, cut through both layers of vine, and remove the excess from each end. Butt ends together and press. Place a leaf over the spliced vine so you can not see the splice.

Vine segments make rings as in these two "Promise Ring" quilts. Use your vine segments for off shoots off a main vine as in the "Tulip Vine" quilt. (p. 68) The flexibility of the vine allows you to keep the vine in the same shape as the template, or you can adjust the vine to make the shape you desire.

You may choose to make vines from bias strips, ribbon, cording, rick rack, or other materials. If so, use your Leaves Galore template to mark a chalk line where you want your vine to be centered. Center the vine material over the line and stitch as desired.

Promise Ring by Joanne Bertrand, Unquilted

Promise Ring by Sue Pelland

CHAPTER 5:
Cutting Fabric Frames

Redwork Frames by Elaine Nadeau: Antique redwork blocks, fused frames, machine appliquéd, hand quilted

CUTTING FRAMES

Frames for appliquéd, pieced, or embroidered blocks can be made with the Leaves Galore templates. By using the snowflake method (fold fabric then cut) we can make symmetrical frames with just one cut with a rotary cutter.

This redwork quilt is surrounded by frames rotary cut with the Petite template.

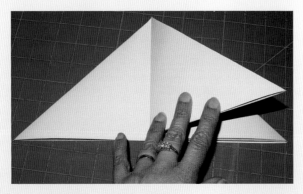

Different looks can be achieved by varying the size of the squares, the location of the cut, and the size of the template. Experimenting with your options on paper is the best way to find a frame that you like for your project. Even frames with sharp points in the corners are not difficult to stitch as in "Redwork Frames".

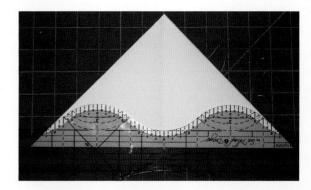

Here, I made a paper frame to ensure that the redwork designs fit inside the cut frame. Notice how the template is lined up with the center fold of the top triangle. On the ends the frame will come to a sharp point as in the finished redwork quilt. The piece that you cut out of the center of the frame is a valuable shape and can be used for alternating block design quilts.

Frames for quilts are not made from a square of fabric as this would be a huge waste of fabric. Instead, make frames for large squares or quilts by fusing four curved borders and mitering the ends. See the Step by Step instructions for making large frames.

Once you try one exercise in making a frame, you can imagine all the possibilities.

Basic Frame Instructions:
Step by Step

STEP 1: Decide on the outside frame measurement (finished size of the block).

STEP 2: Draw a line on the back of the fabric at least 1½" from the fabric edge on all four sides. This is the line on which you will center the fusible and center the template for cutting. Measure the resulting square.

STEP 3: Cut four strips of fusible for each block the length of the inside square. There is no need to put fusible on the entire block and you don't want fusible within the seam allowances between blocks. Center your fusible on the marked line (Mistyfuse works great as you can see right through it!) and apply fusible strips with an appliqué pressing sheet. You can overlap the strips, as Mistyfuse is so soft, even two layers is fine. Wait for 15 minutes after applying fusible.

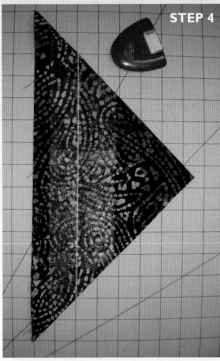

STEP 4: Fold the frame square in quarters along diagonal lines with right sides together. Mark a chalkline at least 1½" from the edge.

STEP 5: Fold the top triangle in half to find the center of the resulting triangle. Center the desired curve vertically on the chalk line and horizontally on the fold line. Cut carefully from edge to edge using a very sharp rotary cutter blade.

STEP 6: Unfold frame. Both center and frame are edged with fusible and can be applied to another fabric. Complete decorative machine stitching along the inside of the frame with stitching falling on the top fabric. These blocks can be used as alternating blocks in a quilt.

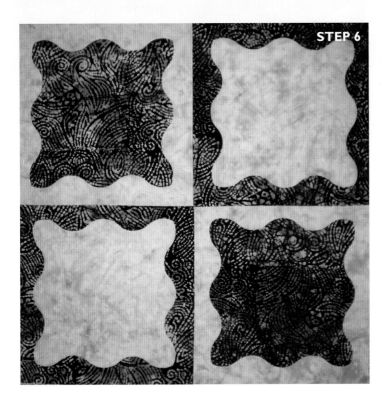

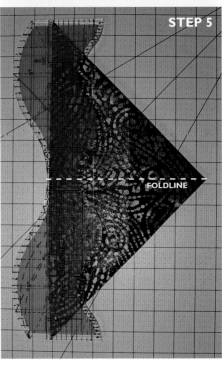

Frames for Quilts: Step by Step

STEP 1: Cut two fabrics for the border, four light borders and two dark borders. Dark borders are slightly longer than light borders. Fold the borders in half lengthwise and crease.

STEP 2: Center a 2" wide strip of fusible on the crease line of the dark borders. Cut down the center of the fusible, keeping centering line of curve on center fold of border.

STEP 3: Fold the cut borders in half to find the center. Line up the peaks of the curves on the light border by placing either a peak or a valley on the center line. Fuse, and trim off excess.

STEP 4: Fold all four borders in half keeping the curves symmetrical around the fold. Use a light box to make sure your curves are symmetrical around the fold. Make sure you are centered either on an inside or outside curve. Mark the center fold with a pin.

STEP 5: Fold quilt to find the center of each side of the quilt.

STEP 6: Pin borders to quilt matching centers.

STEP 7: Sew from center out on each border, stopping ¼" before the end of the seam and back stitch. You are leaving ¼" open on each end. Press seams toward quilt top away from border.

STEP 8: Miter the ends of your border: Fold the quilt in half along the diagonal, lining up two adjacent borders so they lay flat and even along the outside edges. Place a pin through the very last stitch through both layers and pin toward outside of border.

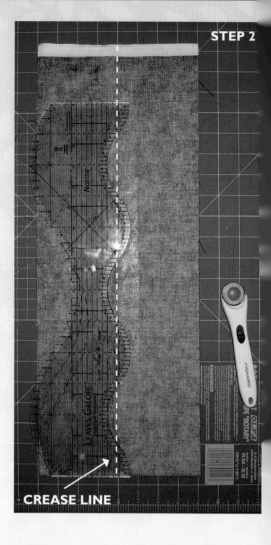

STEP 2

CREASE LINE

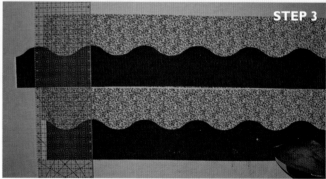

STEP 3

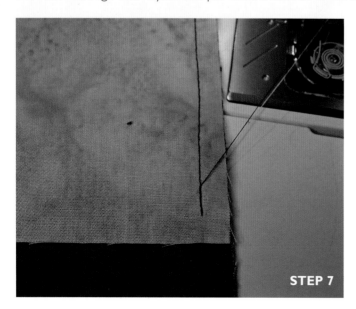

STEP 7

STEP 7

36

STEP 9: Using a ruler, mark a 45 degree angle starting at the pin and leaning toward the right. Turn the quilt over and mark the second border in the same way.

STEP 10: Using a second pin, place the pin on the marked line exactly where the curve crosses the marked line. You will need to look on the right side of the border to ensure you have the pin exactly between the two fabrics. Place the tip of the pin into the second border, exactly where the curve crosses the line.

STEP 11: Stitch on the diagonal line, starting exactly where your last stitch ended. Backstitch. Continue sewing line to the outside edge of the border. Backstitch.

STEP 12: Press seam open and inspect corner. Adjust as needed. Trim to ¼" beyond stitching and press seam open. Repeat Steps 8 to 11 to complete all four corners.

STEP 13: Stitch the appliqué with a decorative machine stitch.

STEP 10

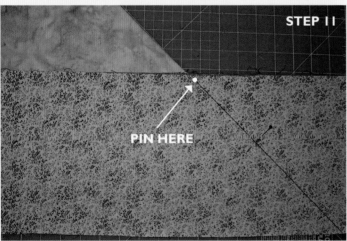

STEP 11

PIN HERE

STEP 12

CHAPTER 6:
Creating Fabric

Remembering Monet's Garden by Sue Pelland

CREATING FABRIC

Fabric for quilt tops or blocks can be created using one or more of the template edges to create curvy rows of various fabrics. The resulting fabric can be a quilt top by itself (think ocean waves or landscapes) or can be cut up into various shapes for piecing or borders.

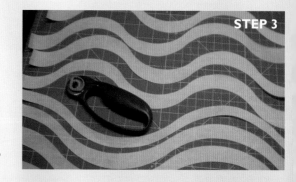

Creating Curvy Fabric: Step by Step
Method One: Raw Edges

STEP 1: Cut fabric strips of various widths between 6" and 8" wide.

STEP 2: Fold each strip in half lengthwise.

STEP 3: Cut strips of PAPER BACKED fusible with the curve you choose, one inch wide by width of fabric, just as you would cut a vine. (p. 22)

This is the only time you would use paper-backed fusible for my techniques. You will need a one inch strip for each strip of fabric.

STEP 4: Center the paper backed fusible curvy strip on the center line of the fabric strip. (photo shows two strips with different size curves)

STEP 5: Cut the fabric strip in half using the curve down the center of the paper backed fusible strip resulting in two curved edge pieces each with a ½" of fusible on the curvy edge.

STEP 6: Remove paper backing from each strip.

STEP 7: Starting from the top, lay one full strip on your pressing surface then place one of the cut curves over the first strip. Press in place.

STEP 8: After layering the first curve, cut away the excess fabric from the first strip where it falls below the fused curve.

STEP 9: Add a new curve below the first curve placing them in a random and eye pleasing pattern.

STEP 10: Keep adding new layers until your fabric or quilt top is an appropriate size. Stitch with decorative stitching along each edge.

STEP 11: Cut into borders or squares as needed for project. The fabric pictured in Step 10 was used to make the border for "Katherine's Quilt".

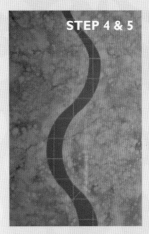
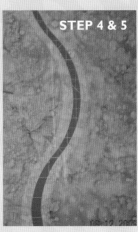

STEP 4 & 5   STEP 4 & 5

STEP 10

Background for "Remembering Monet's Garden" was made with Method One. Three fabric panels were created, each shaded from light to dark. Decorative machine stitching was completed on each panel in long lines from edge to edge of the fabric. Fabric panel was cut into 8½" squares and joined together to make the backing. Water lilies (p. 29) were added randomly and fused on the fabric panel then sewn with a straight stitch along the edges of the flowers.

Katherine's Quilt by Sue Pelland

Creating Curvy Fabric:
Step by Step

Method Two: Edges Finished with Piping, Trim, or Lace.

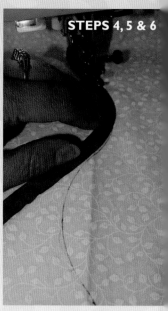

STEP 1: Trim piping to have a ¼" seam allowance. I use the Piping Hot Binding tool.

STEP 2: Cut fabric strips of various widths between 6" and 8" wide.

STEP 3: Reserve one strip that will be the top edge of your curved fabric.

STEP 4: Fold remaining strips in half lengthwise and crease to mark the center line.

STEP 5: Place template over the center line and draw a curve from edge to edge of the strip on the right side of the fabric.

STEP 6: Place piping, trim, or lace edge along marked curve line. Sew ¼" away from the marked curve to attach piping or trim using a zipper foot or piping foot on your machine.

STEP 7: Add second row of piping or trim with raw edge on the curved line. Sew with ¼" seam.

STEP 8: Cut on the curved line between two rows of piping or trim, resulting in two curvy strips.

STEP 9: Turn piping or trim to right side of fabric and press so raw edges fold under to the back side of the curved strip. You will end up with two curved strips each with a finished edge.

STEP 10: Finish all strips of fabric in this manner.

STEP 11: Lay reserved strip on a flat surface. Lay curved edge strip over first strip with curved edge on top. Pin strip two to strip one. Stitch in the ditch between the strip fabric and the piping. Trim excess fabric behind second strip ¼" below stitching line.

STEP 12: Add a new curve below the first curve placing them in a random and eye pleasing pattern.

STEP 13: Keep adding new layers until your fabric or quilt top is an appropriate size.

"Cape Cod" was made with Method Two. Fabrics with contrasting piping were then stitched in the ditch between the piping and each additional layer. The final layer was made with glittered tulle and appliquéd raw edge (Method One) over the golden sand fabric to resemble the bubbly edge of the wave washing up on the sand. Sea Gulls were added by folding fused fabric and cutting the gulls with the 2.5" edge of the Petite template.

"Chromosomes 9 and 22" was also made with Method Two. Strip pieced panels were marked with the 8" curve, edged with thick black piping, then cut and rearranged. The quilts represent the defective chromosomes that cause Chronic Mylogenous Leukemia. The Leaves Galore templates are orange, the color of the Leukemia awareness ribbon. This quilt celebrates my son's remission and constant struggle with CML.

Cape Cod by Sue Pelland

Chromosomes Nine and Twenty Two by Sue Pelland

CHAPTER 7:
Finishing Stitches for Appliqué

Sweet Summer Vine by Joanne Bertrand, Quilted by Debbie Wendt

Generally I enclose the edge of the fusible appliqué using a decorative machine stitch for any quilt that will get washed repeatedly in its lifetime. While fusible products are wonderful to use, I do not want to rely on this bond during washing. Lets consider the fusible to be a temporary bond that gets us through the next few phases of making the quilt. Stitching is the most important step in any quilt.

There are many ways to finish the edges of your fusible appliqué depending on the end use and the look you desire. Decorative stitching, couching, and straight stitching are all good ways to finish your appliqué.

On the right are four examples of edge treatments that I tried before making "Mint

Chocolate" quilt (p. 79). Decorative stitching was done first before piecing the beige backgrounds. There are a number of decorative stitches on modern machines. If your machine is an older model or a basic machine, try a simple zigzag stitch (Photo 1). If your machine offers many choices, try out a few stitches before you settle on one for your quilt. I often choose a traditional buttonhole stitch (photo 2) but also really love the feather stitch in this example (photo

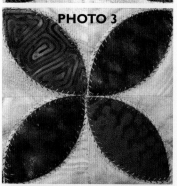

3). When using the star stitch (Photo 4) it was difficult to keep the straight stitches between stars on the edge of the leaf patches. For "Mint Chocolate" (p. 78) I opted for the buttonhole stitch.

Decorative stitching along the edge, even if it is a straight quilting stitch, can be made more decorative by using a heavier weight thread or a contrasting thread color. I love variegated threads. They are a great choice when your quilt contains many colors of appliqué and you don't want to change threads with each patch.

To make stitching "disappear", use a matching thread or a very lightweight thread that "melts" into the appliqué colors or prints.

When ending decorative machine stitching, bring both thread ends to the back of the fabric. Tie off ends. Put two ends through a large eye needle and weave ends into the last several stitches before trimming ends close to stitching. This will secure thread ends and eliminate dark thread ends showing through light background fabrics.

Couching is another way to finish some types of appliqué. The shapes in "Magic Carpet Ride" (p. 60) lend themselves to couching. When you can do one long continuous line of stitching from one edge of the quilt to the other you can couch yarn or decorative threads over the edges of your appliqué. Couching was an excellent choice for this quilt made of blue jeans. The thick yellow thread couched over the raw edges of the jean material creates a strong visual line while helping to hide the raw edges of the denim. Notice that the shape is made by cutting both sides of the Grande Leaves Galore template. The addition of couched, random vertical lines adds interest and distracts the eye so you don't notice that all the

Jeans Quilt by Marilyn Ferkinhoff

appliquéd curves are made with only the 8" and 4" curves.

Straight stitching along the edges of each appliqué patch is another good option for decorative stitching. Straight stitching does not enclose the edge or camouflage fraying like couching does. Straight stitching should only be chosen if you can accept that fraying may occur along the edges of the raw edge patches. The patches will only fray to the stitched line, so keep your stitching close to the edges and reduce possible fraying. "Tulip

Vine" (p. 68) was stitched before quilting using a free motion foot. Just as in quilting, free motion sewing with your feed dogs down allows you to move in any direction to secure your appliqué patches to the background fabric. This reduces the twisting and turning that would need to happen using a standard straight stitch and your feed dogs up. Sew around each appliqué element using a matching thread. Bring threads to back of your work, tie off, and weave into last few stitches before trimming.

Depending on the quilt, I sometimes quilt and appliqué all at one time. This is only possible on small quilts crib size or less. After fusing the pieces in place, add borders to finish the quilt top. Layer and baste for quilting. Match top thread to appliqué and bobbin thread to quilt backing. Stitch with decorative machine stitches through all three layers. This is only recommended if you don't mind seeing the decorative stitch on the back of the quilt, however, it is an efficient and simple way to get your quilts done quickly.

If you choose to do a straight stitch instead of a decorative machine stitch, the back looks as good as the front, and your quilting and appliqué can be done at the same time. The straight stitch appliqué allows me to nail down long skinny leaves right to the very tip of the point. This will reduce fraying of the points and allow you to

appliqué sharp points which are not possible with hand appliqué.

When you begin or end decorative stitching through all three layers, you must bring the bobbin thread up to the top of your work to eliminate messes on the back of your work. After completing the decorative stitch, tie off the thread ends. Using a large eye needle, thread both threads through the eye of the needle then pull the threads between the layers of the quilt for one to two inches and come up on the surface with your needle. Pop the small knot through the top layer of fabric so the knot and the thread ends are buried in the batting. Trim threads very close to the surface.

"Hope's Batik Diamond" was machine appliquéd and quilted in one step.

Hope's Batik Diamond by Sue Pelland

CHAPTER 8:
Quilt Finishing: Quilting Designs made with Leaves Galore Templates

Quilting Sampler by Sue Pelland

I used to hand quilt. Then again, I used to hand appliqué! There will never be enough time to make all the quilts I plan to make if I continue to make them all by hand. With limited quilting time, I choose to machine quilt those pieces that have fusible appliqué. It is simple to design quilting patterns to complement appliqué designs when you use the same tools to do both jobs. The Leaves Galore templates are not only cutting tools, they are quilt marking tools as well.

CAN I USE THE TEMPLATES FOR LONG ARM QUILTING?

Leaves Galore templates are very useful tools for marking quilting designs but the 1/8" thickness is not deep enough for use as a long-arm quilting tool. Nevertheless, many long-arm quilters are using my tools. Two Leaves Galore templates of

the same size can be attached together with clear packing tape. The two templates together are ¼" thickness and all the markings that quilters need for guided machine quilting are clearly visible. Fold one edge of the packing tape back on itself to create a handle to remove the tape when needed. This way you can use one template for cutting and two together for long-arm quilting.

USING THE TEMPLATES TO MARK CONTINUOUS LINE DESIGNS

I quilt on my domestic sewing machine, an Elna Excellence 740. The three patterns on page 46 were created by the curved edges of the templates and need to be marked on the fabric. The gentle curves are perfect for quilting on a domestic machine, particularly one with an integrated dual feed system like my Elna. The curves are graceful enough to follow with a walking foot making neat, even stitches.

It is best to mark sections of the quilt top as you go rather than do all the planning ahead of time. There is a lot of movement of the quilt top through the sewing machine that can rub off the marked lines. If you mark too far ahead you may lose your lines.

The first step in marking most quilting designs is to put down a grid on the fabric using a Quilter's Chalk Line and a pattern cutting board. The grid keeps the curved lines both parallel and perpendicular.

Use any of the marking tools (p. 14) or use your favorite marking tool to mark curves. Center your curves over the grid lines using the lines on the template. Mark as closely as possible along the edge of the template. Use the brush off chalk that comes with the tool, or fill with iron-erasable chalk. Most of the chalk will rub off by the time you are finished quilting but you can easily remove excess chalk with a microfiber cloth.

The Bohin Mechanical Chalk Pencil can be used to make lines that last longer. On light colored fabrics you can use the Hera Marker. This tool makes a crease line as you rub it over your fabric. Hold it like you would your rotary cutter as you slide it along the curved edge of the template. There are no chalk lines to remove after quilting. The Chalk Wheel with iron-away chalk works well

on any fabric colors except white (the iron-erase chalk is only available in white). For white quilts, mark with a water erasable pen or the Hera Marker. The Leaves Galore templates give you a variety of overall quilting patterns that you can use as fillers.

Each of the quilting samples in the next column started with a 3" grid. Each was marked with the 3" curve. They are made from either adding or subtracting lines from the basic Orange Peel pattern. The entire set of three Leaves Galore templates can make each of these patterns in six different sizes. While the 5", 6", or 8" string of leaves, clam shell, or orange peel may seem a

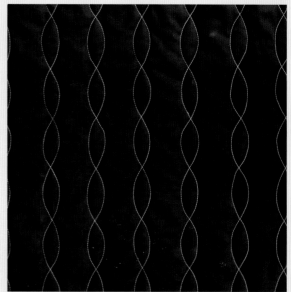

String of Leaves

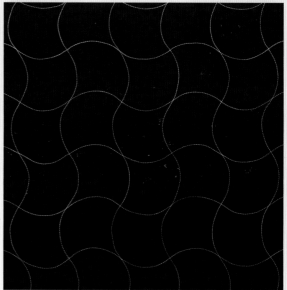

Clamshell

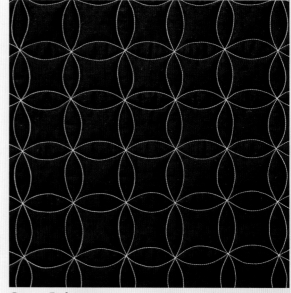

Orange Peel

little large, you can use this pattern as a starting point. Fill the centers of the designs with stippling, feathers, or other suitable design as in the "Orange Peel" quilt below.

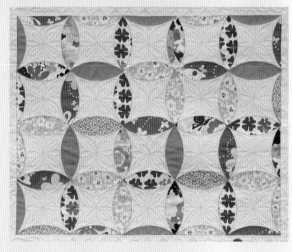

Melissa's Quilt by Sue Pelland

Pieced quilts are based on grids already so you can skip marking your grid with the Quilter's Chalk Line. The sample (p. 48, Photo 1) is pieced with 3" squares. The 3" Norme template was used to mark an Orange Peel design. The curves are centered over the seam lines between blocks.

Examples of quilting designs made with the Leaves Galore templates are in the Appendix (p. 95 and 96). You can make each design with any of the templates resulting in six different sizes.

This is just a sampling of the designs that can be made by experimenting with the templates. Use one section of the design for a border or lay designs side by side to create "all over" patterns. You can often interlock the curves to improve the flow of an all over design. These edge to edge, continuous line patterns are easily quilted using a long-arm quilting machine or can be stitched with a domestic machine using a walking foot.

Quilting designs made with the Leaves Galore templates are easily marked using a Chalk Wheel filled with iron-erase chalk or favorite quilt marking tool. Even though you are not going to iron the quilt after quilting, the iron-erase chalk is advantageous when machine quilting. It is not a mineral based product which is abrasive in your sewing machine. If there is a little chalk left after quilting, brush it away with a soft baby toothbrush or a microfiber cleaning cloth.

DO YOU PIECE YOUR BATTING?

My recommendation is to stitch the edges of your batting together when you piece a batting. Sometimes this results in a visible straight line where the batting was pieced. A better way to splice your batting is to cut a gentle serpentine line instead of a straight line. The curved joint will be less noticeable than a straight line. Free cut the serpentine, or use one of the templates to cut the batting. Overlap the batting edges by 2". Place the template so it touches the batting edge that is on top. Cut your serpentine line with any of the template curves. Remove the excess batting from both the top and the bottom piece so batting edges just touch. Overcast the edge using a thin white thread and loose stitches or use a batting joint tape that irons on. A small strip every inch will keep the batting edges from shifting apart.

FEATHER QUILTING

Front after marking

Back after quilting

Use the curves as spines for feathers. The same principles apply for turning corners on feathers as in Chapter 9 (p. 49), Vines, Serpentine and Scalloped Edges. Once spine is marked draw guidelines on each side of spine to keep feathers a consistent width. Stitch the spine either with or without the walking foot. Switch to free motion quilting and work the feather from front to back. Think of drawing half a heart beginning and ending on your stitched spine. Once one side of the spine is filled with half hearts, start the other side, again, working from front to back. Do not try to match the other feathers to create perfect hearts. Instead, keep these half hearts independent of the others. You will never be able to match the starting and stopping points especially as you round the corners. Keep a similar size and shape to the half hearts on each side of the spine.

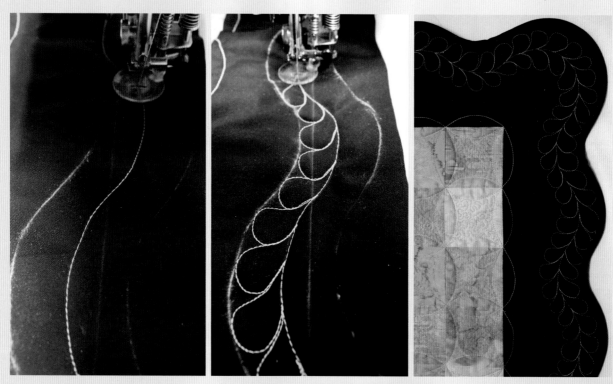

CHAPTER 9:
Vines, Serpentine and Scalloped Edges

Serpentine Melissa's Quilt by Sue Pelland

The Leaves Galore template is the perfect tool for adding vines, scalloped edges, or serpentine edges to your quilts. The difficulty with adding these elements is that there is a certain amount of math that has to happen before you determine which size template to use.

In this book, the math has been done so you can easily determine which template to use to finish the edges of your quilts. There are three tables in the Appendix to assist you. Table 8 (p. 84) is called "Template Multiples" which gives you the exact measurement for different multiples of the templates. When planning a quilt, use this chart to plan the exact size of the quilt, so there is no fudging the edges to get a vine, serpentine, or scalloped edge to fit exactly.

You may already have a quilt that you may want to finish with a vine, serpentine, or scalloped edge. Table 9 in the Appendix (p. 85) is called "Serpentine Edge Quilts and Vines." This table will help you fit any size quilt by letting you know exactly how much fudging you will have to do to get your vine or serpentine edge to fit. Table 10 (p. 90) is called "Scalloped Edge Quilts".

The easiest way to adjust your vine, serpentine, or scalloped edges is to make them out of paper or muslin to fit to your quilt. Another way is to mark directly on the quilt with brush away or iron away chalk. Quilts should be completely quilted before fitting a serpentine or scalloped edge to the quilt.

Serpentine edges have an odd number of inside plus outside curves. Look at your template: Each template has an odd number of curves on the larger side of the template. As on the large side of each template, the serpentine edge will be most attractive when it begins and ends with a full rounded curve.

Table 9 and 10 in the Appendix are designed for serpentine and scalloped edge quilts with full curves on each end of the quilt resulting in a rounded corner. Instructions are only given for a full rounded corner, however, that there are many ways to turn the corners other than the full rounded corner.

Serpentine edges are much easier to finish than scalloped edges. Unlike scalloped edges, there are no inside points or corners to turn. There is one long, graceful, continuous curve around all four sides of your quilt.

A scalloped edge can have any number of scallops and does not need to have an odd number of repeats. For this reason, the scallop is easier to fit to any size quilt and there will be less fudging to make it fit. However, the binding will be more challenging to apply by machine and finish by hand. My preference is to use a serpentine edge whenever possible unless your quilt requires a scalloped edge.

Mark a vine, serpentine, or scalloped edge on your quilt: Step by Step

STEP 1: Draw a straight chalk line on all four edges of your quilt where you want your vine, serpentine, or scalloped edge to fall. This chalk line is most easily marked using a Quilter's Chalk Line as you can snap one line for the entire length or width of your quilt. Lay your quilt out on a carpeted floor and place a large square template where you want your vine, scalloped, or serpentine edge to turn the corner. *Make sure your corner square is at least 1½" in from the edge of your quilt* for a serpentine or scalloped edge, and more than 2" in for vine placement. Place a T-pin into the carpet to anchor one end of the chalk line while you stretch the line across your quilt. Hold the line taut and snap a chalk line. Mark all four straight lines so that they run along the sides of the square template ensuring an exact 90 degree angle at each corner.

STEP 2: Measure the length of the straight line from corner to corner where the lines intersect. Measure both the length and width of the quilt.

STEP 3: Find the numbers on Table 9 or 10 in the Appendix. Choose the Table for either serpentine edges or vines, or for scalloped edges. Read across the appropriate table to find which template(s) work for each number. Find one template that works for both numbers, even if you have to stretch or reduce a certain number of curves. (See Example, p. 52)

STEP 4 (optional): Make a false border using these measurements. Make a border pattern using paper towel or drawing paper roll, freezer paper, adding machine tape, parchment paper, or inexpensive muslin. Cut the pattern the same width as the actual border. Cut one pattern the length of your quilt and one pattern the width of the quilt. Measure 1½" from the edge of this paper or muslin border and mark with pencil. Find the line on the template that bisects the curve and place it on the marked line so the curve is equal above and below the line. Cut the curve on the false border. Place the border pattern over the quilted quilt. Once the corners are turned in a pleasing way, fudge the rest of the curves to fit into the border. Either reduce or stretch the indicated number of curves by ½" each time. Once you have adjusted the curves on the paper or muslin and they fit perfectly on your quilt, mark the cut edge of the border pattern on the actual quilt.

STEP 5: Mark actual border with template using a Chalk Wheel or your favorite marking tool. My tool of choice is the Chalk Wheel (p. 13) filled with iron-erase chalk. Whether you are marking a quilt top or a finished quilt, you can easily remove the iron-off chalk with your iron or a microfiber cloth.

Place the flat end of the template on the marked corner line. Place the centering line of the curve on the chalk line perpendicular to the straight end. Mark with a Chalk Wheel or other removable marking tool. Start marking at both corners of the quilt and end each with a full curve. Move template down the quilt, matching curves to continue the serpentine line. Adjust as needed according to the chart either stretching or reducing desired number of curves by ½". Continue around all four sides in this manner. Continue below for vine, serpentine, or scalloped edge quilts.

CENTERING A VINE ON THE MARKED LINE

❧ Once you have marked the placement curve, the vine must be centered on this line. Place your template on the marked curve.

❧ Slide the template to the left by half the width of the vine. If you have cut a ½" wide vine, slide the template ¼" to the left of the marked line.

❧ Place the cut vine along the edge of the template to help keep the curve consistent.

❧ Splice sections of vine to make one continuous vine around the entire quilt.

❧ For another option, use vines just on the corners or just in the center of your borders instead of a continuous vine around all four sides.

BINDING A SERPENTINE EDGE QUILT

❧ After marking the serpentine edge, place the raw edges of your bias binding (see box) against the marked line.

❧ Stitch with ¼" seam allowance to the left of the marked line using your ¼" foot to get an exact ¼" seam.

❧ Cut the edges of your quilt to match the raw edges of the binding. Use the appropriate template to cut the quilt. The curves may no longer be exactly like the Leaves Galore template but will be close enough so you can use the template and your rotary cutter to cut along marked lines. Be very careful!! Do not cut the quilt before you apply the binding as the edges are likely to stretch. The stitching will act as a stabilizer so the serpentine edge does not stretch.

❧ Turn the binding to the back side of the quilt and hand stitch along the machine stitched line enclosing the raw edges of the binding and quilt.

Sweet Summer Vine with scalloped edge

The Promise of Christmas by Shari Cronin

BIAS BINDING

Serpentine and scalloped edge quilts have to be bound with a bias binding. There are a few different methods of cutting a bias binding, but the one I prefer can be cut with a rotary cutter. Most bias methods start with a square of fabric, but this method can use any size piece of fabric. One half yard of fabric will make four yards of binding.

Starting with a rectangle, fold over one corner to find a 45 degree angle. Cut on fold. Add the triangle that you cut off to the opposite side of the rectangle to form a parallelogram. Sew with a ¼" seam and press the seam open.

Now cut along the bias edge of the parallelogram with a straight acrylic template and a rotary blade. Cut bias strips to desired width for binding. Pin ends of strips right sides together and sew ¼" seams to make one long continuous strip of binding. Press seams open.

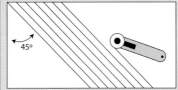

Cut triangle from this edge   *Sew to this edge with ¼" seam*

BINDING A SCALLOPED EDGE QUILT

❧ After marking serpentine edge, slide template down by one full curve and mark additional outside curves to make a scalloped edge.

❧ "Stay stitch" (straight stitch) a scant ¼" in from the marked line using a walking foot on your machine. This stitch will act as a stabilizer so your edges will not stretch while putting on your binding.

❧ Using the template and a sharp 28mm rotary cutter blade, trim the quilt just to the marked line.

❧ Trim inside point to within one or two threads of the ¼" seam line. Do not cut past "stay stitching" line.

❧ Place the two raw edges of your bias binding (see box on page 51) on the raw edge of the quilt and stitch with a generous ¼" seam. As you come to each inside corner, stitch just to the corner and keep your needle in the down position.

❧ With the needle down, lift presser foot and twist the quilt and binding so you can line up the raw edges of the quilt and binding. Smooth with your fingernail all the way up to the needle.

❧ Put presser foot down and stitch around next scallop ending exactly on inside point. Repeat.

❧ Turn the binding to the back side of the quilt and hand stitch along the machine stitched line enclosing the raw edges of the binding and quilt.

EXAMPLE 1: Make a Serpentine Edge on a Crib Size Quilt

From Table 7, (p. 84) you will find that a crib size comforter measures 36" x 54".

TABLE 7: STANDARD QUILT SIZES IN INCHES

Measurement in inches	Mattress top	Comforter	Bedspread	Standard batting size
Crib	28 x 52	36 x 54	DNE	45 x 60

To make a serpentine edge, mark a chalk line 1½" away from each edge on the quilt giving you room to have the curve rise above and dip below the line. The inside lines measure 33" and 51" after taking 1½" away from each edge.

Now look at Table 9 (p. 85) on the row for 33" and 51" lengths:

TABLE 9: SERPENTINE EDGE QUILTS AND VINES

Border Length	2.5"	3"	4"	5"	6"	8"
33	Stretch 1/13	Exact (11)	Reduce 6/9	Reduce 4/7		Stretch 2/4
51	Stretch 3/21	Exact (17)	Reduce 2/13	Reduce 8/11	Reduce 6/9	

This shows that you can either use the 2.5", 3", 4", or 5" templates to make a serpentine edge. Do not use the 6" or the 8" template because these would be too big in scale for the small crib size comforter and there is no data for two of these measurements. If you use the 2.5" template, you will have to stretch one of the 13 curves by ½", and three of the 21 curves by ½".

Using the 3" template, you will have exactly 11 curves on the width, and 17 curves on the length. Both the 4" curves and 5" curves can be used but there will be many adjustments. I recommend using the 3" curve as it is the one with the least number of adjustments.

EXAMPLE 2: Make a Scalloped Edge on a Queen Size quilt

From Table 7, (p. 84) you will find that a queen size comforter measures 86" x 93".

TABLE 7: STANDARD QUILT SIZES IN INCHES

Measurement in inches	Mattress top	Comforter	Bedspread	Standard batting size
Queen	60 x 80	86 x 93	102 x 112	90 x 108

To make a scalloped edge, mark a chalk line 1½" away from each edge on the quilt giving you room to have the scallops rise above the drawn line. The inside lines measure 83" and 90" after taking 1½" away from each edge.

Now look at Table 10 (p. 90) for the row for 83" and 90"

TABLE 10: SCALLOPED EDGE

Border Length	2.5"	3"	4"	5"	6"	8"
83	S 1/33	R 2/28	R 2/21	R 4/17	R 2/14	S 6/10
90	S 5/35 or R 5/37	Exact (30)	S 4/22 or R 4/23	Exact (18)	Exact (15)	S 4/11

This shows that you can use any template to make a scalloped edge. Choose the best curve for the design of your quilt. My preference would be to use the 5" or 6" curve as there are minimal adjustments that have to be made. For the 5" template, your 83" edge would be marked with 17 scallops and four of those would be reduced by ½" each. The length of your quilt would fit exactly with 18 scallops.

Using the 6" template, you would mark 14 scallops on the width of your quilt, only reducing two of the 14 scallops by ½". The length of the quilt would fit exactly with 15 scallops.

Again, any template could be used but more adjustments would be needed for the 2.5", 3", 4", and 8" curves.

Painted Appliqué, by Kathy Sperino

Hot and Cold Flow, by Kathleen Murphy

Joseph's Coat, by Sue Pelland

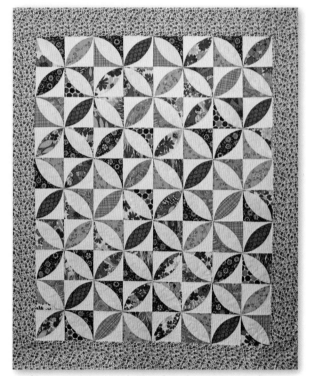

Ruth's Scraps Meet Sue's Template, by Donna Hopkins

Strength & Hope, by Sharon Morris

Elongated Nine Patch, by Glenda Jones, Quilted by Kathy Sperino

Preface

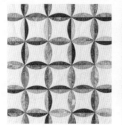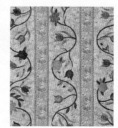

Please read all instructions before beginning the following quilt projects.

ALL PROJECTS REQUIRE:

One or more Leaves Galore templates	Thread to match piecing
6" x 24" acrylic template for straight cutting	Marking pencil or Quilter's Chalk Line
Fusible web of your choice	28mm Rotary Cutter with a brand new blade
Appliqué Pressing Sheet	A new needle in your machine
Thread to match appliqué	Batting

Wash and press fabrics, including background fabrics before using them for appliqué. Review Chapters 3 and 4 for cutting and using appliqué shapes.

Fusing: Tack each shape in place with the tip of an iron. Shapes can then be moved if needed. Cover with pressing sheet and press with hot iron to secure permanently. Turn and press from the back of the panel and use steam to ensure a strong bond.

Quilt finishing: Fine quilt finishing is an art in itself! I recommend getting a good basic quilting book to supplement the information here for basting, quilting, squaring, binding and labeling your quilts.

Square your quilts before binding: Use the Quilter's Chalk Line and a large square template to square up your quilt prior to binding. Instructions are provided in the Chalk Line package.

All quilts can be made with a straight edge, serpentine edge, or scalloped edge. Follow instructions in Chapter 8 for serpentine and scalloped edges. Straight edge quilts can be bound with a straight of grain binding. Yardage requirements are given only for straight bindings. Bias bindings will require extra fabric.

Label your quilts so future generations know for whom, where, and why you made your beautiful appliqué quilts. Important information about the quilt maker would be your first name, last name, maiden name, city, state, and the date. Include both the quilt top maker and the quilter if they are different. I prefer to stitch my label to the backing fabric, then machine or hand quilt through the label so it can not be removed.

Batik Split Orange Peel

42" x 54" | Quilt by Susan Monsegur | Quilted by Susan Pelland

PROJECT 1:
Split Orange Peel

Use the Norme Leaves Galore template

YARDAGE REQUIREMENTS FOR 42" X 54" LAP QUILT

Melons: 9 Fat Quarters
Background: 1½ yards
Binding and Backing: 3 yards
Batting: 44" x 56"
Mistyfuse or 20" wide fusible: 5½ yards

STEP A: PRECUT FABRICS

A1: Cut background fabric into one 38" x 50" panel and four 1½" x 54" strips for inside borders.

A2: Place five fat quarters on your cutting board. Cut two strips 2½" x 22" through all five layers and set aside for outer, pieced border (10 strips).

A3: Cut four strips 3" x 22" through all five layers (20 strips).

A4: Using next four fat quarters, cut one strip 2½" through all four layers and set aside for outer, pieced border (4 strips).

A5: Cut four strips 3" x 22" through all four layers (16 strips).

A6: From the 2½" strips (A2 & A4), cut four strips into eight bars 2½" x 10". These will be used for the ends of the border. Cut the remaining 2½" strips into 2½" x 6½" bars. Save for Step I, Pieced Border.

STEP B: MAKE STRIP SETS

Choose (32) 3" strips. (Steps A3 & A5) Sew long edges together to make four strip sets with eight strips in each set. Sew the strips in random order. Save the remaining strips for partial leaves cut in Step E.

Be sure to eliminate "SMILES". (p. 17, Shape 1B) Do not press until all eight strips are pieced together. This will help eliminate smiles.

STEP C: PRESS STRIP SETS

Press seams open on all four strip sets making sure to keep seams straight. Press fusible web on back of all four strip sets keeping seams open.

STEP D: CUT STRIP SETS INTO 6" LEAVES

Use the cutting instructions for two-toned leaves (p. 17, Shape 1B) to cut 6" leaves. Make sure the center registration line on the 6" template lines up with the seam line every time you cut. Offset leaves on each new seam line. Cut three leaves on each seam line to give 21 leaves from each of the four strip sets, yielding 84 two-toned leaves. Choose 82 of the best leaves for the quilt center.

STEP E: CUT "HALF" LEAVES

Cut 24 partial leaves for the outside edge of the quilt using the remains of the strips sets (Step D). Strip set edges are already fused. Fuse one extra 3" strip (Step B) to get four more partial leaves for a total of 28 partial leaves.

Leaves need to be more than half a leaf. Make sure there is at least ¼" beyond the center leaf marking for seam allowances as shown below.

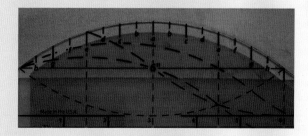

STEP F: MARK GRID

Place background fabric on a pattern cutting board. Leave a one inch border all around grid. Mark a 6" grid, six squares by eight squares with the Quilter's Chalk Line and iron-off chalk powder, or a straight edge and chalk pencil. Do not use any marking tool that will become permanent with pressing such as an air erase or water soluble pen. For white or light backgrounds, you can see the grid through the fabric so there is no need to mark the grid.

Line up split leaves along the marked lines from point to point. Do not cover outside lines. Press the split leaves in place. Press 28 partial leaves from Step E on outer lines.

Give the entire center a good press from the back side using steam.

STEP G: DECORATIVE STITCHING

Complete decorative machine stitch around edges of all leaves.

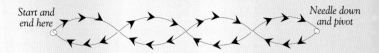

Start and end here   *Needle down and pivot*

STEP H: ADD BORDERS

Sew inside border onto quilt center. Press toward border. Trim outside edges of quilt leaving ¼" beyond outside edge leaf tips. Quilt will measure approximately 36½" x 48½".

STEP I: PIECED BORDER

Using (fourteen) 2½" x 6" bars set aside in Step A6, sew bars end to end to make two rows of four and two rows of six. Press seams to one side. Add 10" bar to both ends of each row.

Sew a row of eight bars on each vertical edge of quilt top, matching seam lines to points of melons. Press toward inside border. Sew a row of seven bars on top and bottom of quilt, centering the border and matching seam lines to melons. Press seams toward inside border.

STEP J: QUILT FINISHING

Layer, baste, quilt, square, bind and label as desired.

Bright Split Orange Peel

42" x 54" | *Quilt by Elaine Nadeau and Susan Pelland | Unquilted, buttonhole through all three layers*

Magic Carpet Ride

This brightly colored quilt was inspired by a Persian carpet
59" x 68" | *Quilt made by Sue Pelland* | *Quilted by Kathy Sperino*

PROJECT 2:
Magic Carpet Ride

Use the Grande Leaves Galore template

YARDAGE REQUIREMENTS FOR 57" X 70" LAP QUILT

Appliqué shapes: ½ yard of 8 fabrics

Background, inner border and binding: 3 yards

Backing: 3.5 yards

Mistyfuse™ or 20" wide fusible: 5 yards

Batting: 66" x 75" or prepackaged twin size

ADDITIONAL SUPPLIES

Thread, yarn, and couching foot if desired.

STEP A: PRE-CUT BACKGROUND FABRIC AND MARK GRID

Cut background fabric 42" x 50". Starting one inch away from each fabric edge, mark grid 3¼" across the width and 8" down the length of the background rectangle. This will give you a one inch border all around the grid. (Diagram 1) Most grid lines are covered with appliqué, but use the Quilter's Chalk Line so grid will be erased with the iron when pressing fusible shapes onto the grid in Step D.

Diagram 1: Layout

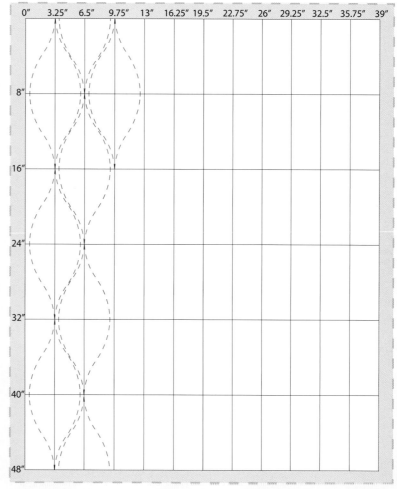

STEP B: PREPARE FABRIC FOR FUSIBLE APPLIQUÉ

Cut three 2½" x WOF (width of fabric) strips from the eight half yard appliqué fabrics. Save for Step I: Piece Piano Key Border. Iron fusible to the back of the remaining fabric pieces.

61

Diagram 2: Cutting

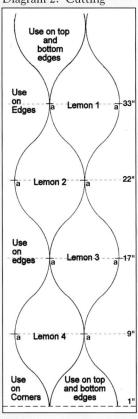

Use on top and bottom edges

Use on Edges — a — Lemon 1 — a — 33"

Lemon 2 — a — 22"

Use on edges — a — Lemon 3 — a — 17"

Lemon 4 — a — 9"

Use on Corners | Use on top and bottom edges — 1"

C: CUT LEMON-SHAPED LEAVES

Stack four appliqué fabrics fusible side down on a cutting mat. Trim bottom edge of fabrics to be even. Place this cut edge on a straight line on the cutting mat to keep template square to fabric. Mark the top fabric with a straight edge and a Chalk Wheel or Chalk Line. Mark a line at 1", 9", 17", 25", and 33" from bottom edge. Starting at the bottom of the WOF, line up the 8" side of the Grande template with the right edge of the fabric. Leave ½" edge to ensure that entire curve is on fabric. Place the "a" line on the template on the one inch mark from the bottom edge of the fabric. The "a" marks on the template will line up with the 1", 9", 17", 22" and 33" lines. Cut with a 28mm rotary cutter from edge to edge. (Diagram 2) Slide template down and to the left until the peaks and valleys meet on the horizontal lines. Make second serpentine cut. Continue with third serpentine cut.

Repeat for second group of four fabrics. You will be able to get four full leaves from each of the eight fabrics, resulting in 32 leaves. Choose the best 28 full leaves for Step D. You will also use the partial leaves on top and bottom of your cuts, and partial leaves on right and left side of the fabrics.

STEP D: ARRANGE LEMON SHAPES ON THE BACKGROUND

You will use 28 full lemons to fill the center of the grid. Starting on the first intersecting chalk lines,

place one full leaf shape over the intersection. Continue to place a leaf on every other chalk line until you have six across. Place another row of six leaves directly below this row (Diagram 1, p. 61). Fill in the spaces between these leaves with a row of five leaves. Repeat for the third and final row. Fill in edges and corners with partial lemon shapes. As long as the shape is ¼" larger than a half lemon, it is useable on the edges. Keep spacing between shapes approximately ½" to ¾" apart, using marked grid lines through the centers of the lemon shapes. Random placement is the easiest way to arrange the colors.

STEP E: TEMPORARY APPLIQUÉ STITCH

Sew the edge of the lemon shapes down in continuous lines from top to bottom of the quilt. There will be about a 1½" space between shapes in each vertical line. Connect the shapes with a line of stitching so you can keep your lines continuous. Use a loose zigzag for the first pass over all the shapes. This keeps the cut edges neat and secure until you can go back and do a second pass with a tight satin stitch or couched yarn.

STEP F: DECORATIVE STITCHING

Use a satin stitch or couching as your final appliqué stitch. Skip to Step G for couching. The satin stitch does take a long time to complete, about 10 minutes for each line, and there are 24 lines of stitching in the lap quilt. This is four hours of stitching! It is worth it in the end.

STEP G: COUCHING OVER RAW EDGE

You can get a similar look to the satin stitch by couching yarns over the raw edge of the appliqué. Couching is done by setting your machine to a loose zigzig, 3.5 length and width on my machine. Using a couching foot, place a matching decorative yarn between the guides on the foot. Hold the yard taut, to guide it between the lines on the foot as you stitch. Do not hold too tightly,

or you will gather up your stitches, just hold firm enough to guide the yarn into the foot. As you zigzag over the yarn, you will cover the raw edges of the lemon shapes. In the space between shapes, lay one yarn beside the other rather than on top of each other.

Couching yarns over the edges is a fast, decorative approach and gives you the opportunity to add another decorative element to the quilt surface. This is best done on quilts that are not to be used every day or washed frequently. Satin stitch is a stronger method of appliqué than couching.

STEP H: ADD INSIDE BORDERS

Use the Quilter's Chalk Line to square up the quilt center to approximately 39½" x 48½'. Now that your stitching is finished, the width measurements may be slightly smaller. Mark chalk lines down the centers of the outside edge

lemons for a stitching line. Cut ¼" beyond the stitching lines on the outside edges for seam allowance.

Cut four strips of fabric 2½" x 48½" long for the inside border. Sew the long vertical borders on first, press toward border. Sew the two horizontal borders on, press toward border. Trim excess.

STEP I: PIECE PIANO KEY BORDER

Strip piece 2½" strips cut in Step "B". Sew eight fabrics in random order to make three sets of eight strips. Cut strip pieced panels into five 8" wide sections. Continue to put segments together until you have two borders 52½" long and two borders 59½" long. Sew Piano Key borders on sides of quilt first, then top and bottom of quilt. Press seam toward solid border.

STEP J: QUILT FINISHING

Layer, baste, quilt, square, bind and label as desired.

Golden Magic Carpet by Joanne Bertrand, Unquilted

Sweet Summer Vine

90" x 113" | Quilt by Sue Pelland & Joanne Bertrand | Quilted by Celine Spader

29" x 29" | Quilt by Joanne Bertrand | Quilted by Debbie Wendt

PROJECT 3:
Sweet Summer Vine

Use the Petite and Norme Leaves Galore template

YARDAGE REQUIREMENTS FOR 29" ONE BLOCK WALL QUILT

Square in a Square Block:

Fabric one: Background for sashing, cornerstones, and center "square in square" block: 1 yard

Fabric two: ¼ yard or 6" square

Fabric three: ⅓ yard or 11" square

Fabric four: ⅓ yard or (2) 10" squares

Appliqué flowers: scraps from "square in a square" or ⅛ yard

Appliqué vines: scraps from "square in a square" or ⅛ yard

Appliqué leaves: scraps equal to ⅛ yard

Backing: 40" square, or 1¼ yards

Binding: 2 strips, 2.5" × WOF (width of fabric) (⅛ yard)

Mistyfuse™ or 20" wide fusible: ¾ yard

Batting: 40" square

STEP A: PRE-CUT FABRICS

"Square in a Square" Block

Fabric two: Cut two squares 5⅜" Cut in half on diagonal

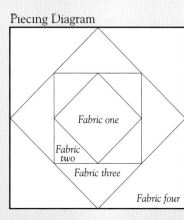

Piecing Diagram

Fabric one

Fabric two

Fabric three

Fabric four

Fabric three: Cut one square 10¼" Cut in half twice on the diagonal to yield four triangles

Fabric four: Cut two squares 9⅞" Cut on diagonal

From the Background Fabric:

Cut two sashing strips, 6½" × WOF. From these two strips cut four 6½" × 18½" sashings. Cut one 7" square for center of "Square in a Square" block. Cut four 6½" corner squares.

STEP B: PREPARE FABRIC FOR FUSIBLE APPLIQUÉ

Iron Mistyfuse to back of flower, leaf, and vine fabrics for appliqué shapes.

STEP C: FINGER PRESS SASHING FABRIC, CORNERSTONES, AND CENTER OF PIECED BLOCK

Mark the center of the sashing strips at 3¼" by folding in half along the length and finger press a light fold down the center. Fold the four cornerstone squares and one 7" square in half and finger press. Fold in half again to divide the square into four quarters. Unfold and repeat along diagonal lines.

STEP D: CUT FLOWER PETALS AND ASSEMBLE FLOWERS

From the flower fabrics cut (40) 2½" standard leaves using the Petite Leaves Galore template.

Using concentric circle diagram (Appendix, p. 97) under appliqué pressing sheet to assemble daisy flowers (p. 29).

STEP E: CUT FUSIBLE VINES

From the fused eighth yard of vine fabric, cut two 18½" lengths. Place each piece fusible side down on cutting mat. Center Norme template (18") long on the 18½" edge of fabric. Cut along edge of template extending cut by ¼" on each end of template. Shift template straight to the left by ³⁄₈" keeping the template centered with ¼" extra fabric on top and bottom. Cut two vines from the two layers of fabric to give four vine segments.

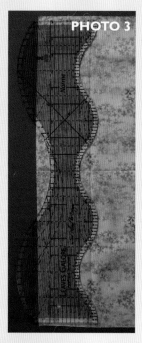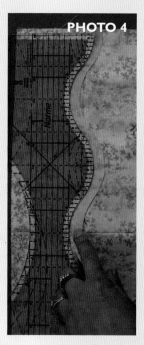

Center vine segments on the sashing strips using the Norme template as your guide.

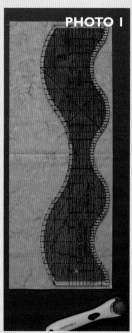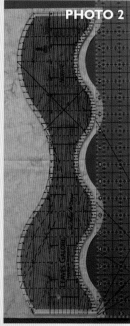

Cutting vine segments with the Norme Leaves Galore template.

STEP F: PLACE FUSIBLE VINES ON SASHING

Place vine segments on sashing strips by using the Norme template as your guide. Center the vine by placing the template approximately ¼" to the left of the finger pressed center line (Photo 3 and 4).

STEP G: DECORATIVE STITCHING: VINES

Sashings: Decorative stitching is done on each element after fusing appliqué in place. I prefer to use a buttonhole stitch and often use variegated threads that match the appliqué colors. For the sashing strips, start at one end of the vine, and as you come to a leaf, go around the leaf then back to the vine and on to the next leaf. This will eliminate the need to start and stop your decorative stitch and eliminate tying off threads on the back of the piece. You can complete each vine with leaves in one continuous stitch without leaving thread tails.

STEP H: DECORATIVE STITCHING: FLOWERS

Complete decorative stitching around all flower petals on both 6½" cornerstones and 7" center blocks. With the flowers being two layers there is not a way to stitch around the entire flower with a decorative stitch without starting and stopping. One method is to start and stop at each end of the half leaves and pull the tail ends of the thread to the back side and tie them off. Then stitch around the N, S, E and W facing petals in one continuous loop. Pull starting and ending threads to the back and tie off.

Another method is to turn your machine to a straight stitch and travel around parts of the appliqué with a straight stitch instead of stopping and starting. This works well as your straight stitching will be covered by the buttonhole stitch as you complete the N, S, E, and W petals.

STEP I: MAKE "SQUARE IN A SQUARE" BLOCK

Starting with the 7" appliqué block, add three sets of four triangles around the edges (Piecing Diagram, p. 65). Fold each triangle to find the center of the long side. Sew each set of four triangles on sides of center square making sure centers match. Make sure block is square after each set of four triangles is added. Size of completed block is 18½".

STEP J: PIECE THE QUILT TOP

Sew two vine segments on each side of finished "square in a square" block. Press toward center square. Sew two flower squares to the ends of the two remaining vine segments. Press seam allowance toward flower squares. Sew two long flower/vine segments to remaining sides of "square in a square" block, matching the seams.

STEP K: QUILT FINISHING

Layer, baste, quilt, square, bind and label as desired.

YARDAGE REQUIREMENTS FOR 90" X 113" QUILT (Pictured on page 64)

Square in a Square Block:
Fabric one: Background for sashing, cornerstones and center "square in square" block: 4¼ yards
Fabric two: 1¼ yards
Fabric three: 3¾ yards
Fabric four: 2½ yards
Appliqué flowers: scraps from "square in a square" or ¼ yard
Appliqué vines: scraps from "square in a square" or ¼ yard
Appliqué leaves: scraps equal to ¼ yard
Backing: 9 yards
Binding: ½ yard
Mistyfuse™ or 20" wide fusible: 1½ yards
Batting: 120" x 120"

Rotary cut:
(228) 2½" flower petals
(186) 2½" leaves
(31) ⅜" vines

🌿 Make (12) 7" center flower blocks and (20) 6½" corner square blocks. (Steps A to D)
🌿 Make 12 "square in a square" blocks. (Step I)
🌿 Make 31 sashing strips. (Steps A to G)
🌿 Sew sashings between each row of three blocks making four rows.
🌿 Make five rows of three sashing strips set with corner blocks.
🌿 Sew rows together. Add two vertical borders then two horizontal borders to appliqué center.
🌿 Proceed with quilt finishing. (Step K)
🌿 90" x 113" finished quilt size. Use the 5" template to make a scalloped edge.

Tulip Vines

79" x 115" | Quilt made by Sue Pelland | Quilted by Diana Annis

PROJECT 4:
Tulip Vines

Use all three Leaves Galore templates

This modern version of an antique row quilt is made current by both techniques and materials. I combined gorgeous batiks with my own rotary cut appliqué designs to make a traditional quilt more modern. Raw edge fused appliqué is complemented by Dianna Annis' stunning long-arm quilting. The quilt in the photo is very long at 79" x 115". A more useable size quilt would end up being 82" x 96" with a straight edge and 79" x 93" with a serpentine edge. Instructions are given for the smaller size quilt. Enough appliqué shapes are cut to make either size quilt. Extra flowers, tulips and leaves give you flexibility when designing your rows, and you will end up with a few extras for a future project.

YARDAGE REQUIREMENTS FOR 79" X 96" QUILT

Background Fabric: 2 yards cut into (3) 14" x 66" strips
Sashing Fabric: 2 yards cut into (4) 6¾" x 66" strips
Top and bottom inside border: 2 yards cut into (2) 6¾" x 66" strips
Outside Border Fabric: 2.5 yards cut into (2) 8½" x 80" and (2) 8½" x 82" strips
Backing: 7½ yards
Batting: 90" x 108"
Mistyfuse or 20" wide fusible: 3 yards

STEP A: FUSE THE FOLLOWING FABRICS TO CUT APPLIQUÉ SHAPES

Pink for tulips, six lobe flowers: Scraps to equal ½ yard

Green for Vine: Fat Quarter, 18" x 22" cut in half to make two 11" x 18" pieces

Blue for six lobe flowers ¼ yard or (3) 6" squares

BlueGreen/Lime prints for tulip leaves (2) ⅛ yard pieces or scraps equal to ¼ yard

Turquoise/Green prints for standard shape leaves including buds: Scraps equal to ¼ yard

STEP B: CUT APPLIQUÉ SHAPES

Rotary cut appliqué shapes (refer to photo for colors and change colors as desired)

Pink tulip centers: Cut 20 standard leaf shapes with the 4" Grande template (p. 15)

Pink tulip petals: Cut 18 "S" shapes and 18 "Z" shapes with the 2½" Petite template (p. 19 and 27)

BlueGreen/Lime for tulip leaves: Cut 18 thin "S" shapes and 18 "Z" shapes with the 5" Petite template from "h" to "h" (p. 27)

Pink bud centers: Cut 15 standard leaf shapes with the 2½" Petite template (p. 15 and 16)

Turquoise/Green bud leaves: Cut 30 standard leaves with the 2½" Petite template. Cut 34 2½" standard leaves with the 2½" Petite template (p. 15 and 16)

Blue and pink six lobed flower fabrics: Cut 6 six-lobed flowers using the flower template (p. 73)

Green vines: Place 11" x 18" fabrics right sides together and cut nine ½" wide vine segments along the 18" edge by centering two 8" curves as shown in Photo 1 and 2 on left. Center the inflection point on the 18" length of fabric by placing the top edge of the template one inch down from fabric edge. Use the lines on your cutting board to help you.

STEP C: FLOWERS
Assemble tulip flowers and buds according to directions on pages 27 and 30.

Diagram 1

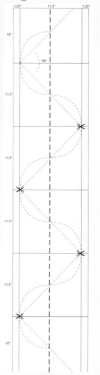

STEP D: MARK BACKGROUND
Place background fabric panel over pattern cutting board and mark iron-erasable chalk line down center of background fabric panels. Mark two lines 1¼" away from each long edge. Measure 10" in from one end then mark a line across the border. Continue to mark every 11½" from that line. This will give you a row of four 11½" squares that are centered on the 14" wide border. Mark a diagonal line across each square in a zigzag fashion. Use a square template to mark a line at a 90 degree angle to the diagonal line in the two end 10" rectangular blocks. Repeat for two more fabric panels. The center panel is rotated 180° to become the mirror image of the two outside panels.

STEP E: FUSE VINES AND FLOWERS
Alternate "Left" and "Right" vines centered on diagonal lines in 11½" squares to form the vine pattern pictured in the quilt photo. Use half vine segments to complete ends of each vine within the 10" section. Vines segments are slightly long and will cross at the corners of each square. Trim vines through both layers where they cross and butt ends of vine. Fuse in place. (Diagram 1

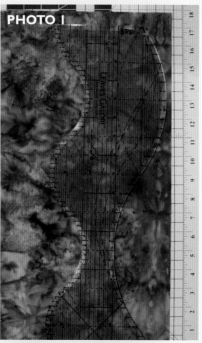

PHOTO 1

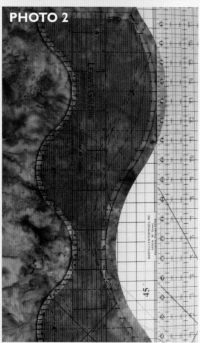

PHOTO 2

and Photo 3) Extra vine segments will be used for side shoots off your main vine. They may be trimmed to be slightly less than ½" wide if desired. Use them for stems of the tulip flowers.

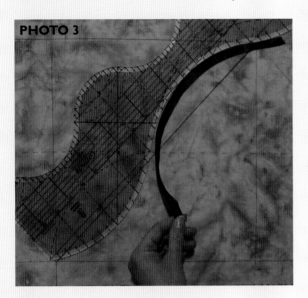

PHOTO 3

STEP F: ASSEMBLE APPLIQUÉ ROWS

Arrange precut flowers, tulips, buds, and leaves along the vine in a pleasing pattern. Use your own creativity in placing the flowers to make this quilt your own, or enlarge the enclosed pattern for placement of flowers and leaves. Fuse in place.

STEP G: DECORATIVE STITCHING

Complete decorative machine stitching as desired around each appliqué shape. Cover quilt (p. 68) shows edge stitching with a straight stitch, matching thread colors to fabric colors. I stitched with a free motion foot just through the quilt top.

STEP H: ADD SASHING AND BORDERS

Sew long sashing strips between rows. Sew top and bottom sashing strips. Sew long borders to left and right side of quilt, followed by top and bottom borders. (Diagram 2)

Diagram 2

		Border one					
Border two	Fabric Stripe Panel or large print	Fabric strip panel or large print				Fabric Stripe Panel or large print	Border two

Fabric strip panel or large print

Fabric Stripe Panel or large print — Appliqué Row — Fabric stripe panel or large print — Appliqué Row — Fabric Stripe Panel or large print — Appliqué Row — Fabric Stripe Panel or large print

Fabic stripe panel or large print

Border one

STEP I: QUILT FINISHING

Layer, baste, quilt, bind and label as desired. Pictured below are two options for a straight edge or a 6" serpentine edge quilt. Instructions for serpentine edge begin on page 49.

Vine Template

Enlarge 147% on a copier. Line up on red lines.

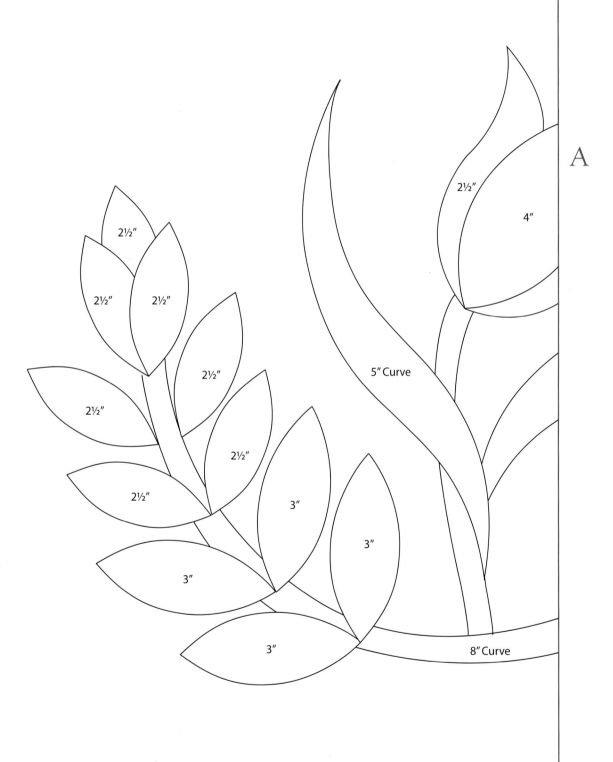

A

8" Curve

5" Curve

2½"

4"

2½"

2½"

2½"

2½"

2½"

2½"

2½"

3"

3"

3"

3"

Vine Template

Enlarge 147% on a copier. Line up on red lines.

A

B

3"

3"

3"

3"

3"

3"

3"

5" Curve

2½"

2½"

5" Curve

5" Curve

3"

3"

Six Lobed Flower

3"

Vine Template

Enlarge 147% on a copier. Line up on red lines.

B

5" Curve

5" Curve

5" Curve

4"

2½"

2½"

3"

3"

3"

2½"

2½"

Vine Template

Enlarge 147% on a copier. Line up on red lines.

3"

3"

3"

D

Six Lobed Flower

3"

4"

2½"

3"

3"

4"

2½"

2½"

2½"

2½"

2½"

2½"

2½"

Vine Template

Enlarge 147% on a copier. Line up on red lines.

D

E

3"

2½"

2½"

4"

5" Curve

5" Curve

5" Curve

5" Curve

2½"

2½"

2½"

5" Curve

2½"

2½"

2½"

Vine Template

Enlarge 147% on a copier. Line up on red lines.

2½"

2½"

2½"

2½"

2½"

2½"

2½"

2½"

2½"

3"

8" Curve

Mint Chocolate

84" x 99" | By Sue Pelland and Joanne Bertrand | Quilted by Celine Spader

PROJECT 5:
Mint Chocolate

Use the Grande Leaves Galore template

YARDAGE REQUIREMENTS FOR 84" X 99" QUILT

Background squares: 6 yards assorted beige to brown prints or scraps to equal 6 yards

Leaves: 14 fat quarters assorted greens/teals or scraps equal to 3.5 yards

Borders: 2.5 yards beige print
3 yards brown print
½ yard teal solid

Binding: 4 strips 2¼" x 108" (cut from the 3 yard length left over from the brown border)

Backing: 6 yards of 42" wide fabric
2¾ yards at 108" wide fabric

Batting: 90" x 108"

Mistyfuse or 20" wide fusible: 7 yards

🌿 Fabric choices for background: Use 24 fat quarters, 12 half yards of fabric or scraps to equal 6 yards of fabric. My fabrics range from beige to dark chocolate brown. The more fabrics the better, making your colors flow from light in the center of the quilt to dark on the edges.

🌿 Fabric choices for leaves: Use 14 fat quarters or any combination of scraps to equal 3½ yards of fabric. The leaf fabrics are not graded from light to dark.

STEP A: PRE-CUT FABRICS

Cut borders and binding as follows:

Two @ 1" x 74" Teal and 2 @ 1" x 88" Teal

Two @ 3" x 74" Beige and 2 @ 3" x 88" Beige

Two @ 6" x 86" Brown and 2 @ 6" x 100" Brown

Four @ 2¼" x 108" Brown (binding)

Cut 644 3³/₈" background squares from beige to brown fabrics.

STEP B: PREPARE FABRICS FOR FUSIBLE APPLIQUÉ

Apply fusible to back of all leaf fabrics. Cut 644 4" standard leaves using 4" side of Grande template.

STEP C: FUSE LEAVES TO SQUARES

Center leaves on diagonal of square, making sure there is exactly ¼" around the ends of the leaves.

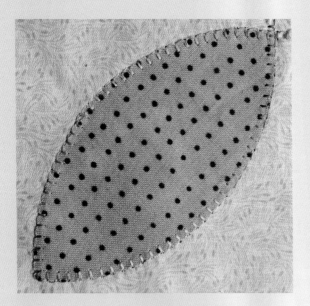

STEP D: DECORATIVE STITCHING

Stitch leaves with a decorative machine stitch.

STEP E: ARRANGE SQUARES

Once all leaves are appliquéd, arrange background squares from dark on outside edges, to a very light center with a grid of 23 × 28 squares. Lay the background squares on the back of a flannel tablecloth or on design wall. Flannel tablecloths make a great design wall, and the squares really stick to the backing. You can tape this on a wall with painter's tape to view the gradation from a distance. Rearrange squares as desired.

STEP F: PIECE CENTER PANELS

Stitch squares together first into horizontal rows. Press seams in each row in one direction, alternating direction with each new row. Sew rows together into one center panel, 66.125" × 80.5".

STEP G: ADD BORDERS

Measure quilt top in each direction and cut two borders to the exact length each time you add two borders. This will ensure a square and flat

quilt with no rippled borders. Press each toward outside edge of quilt.

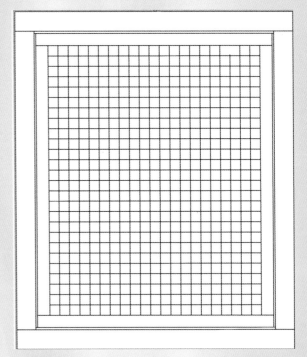

Mint Chocolate, Full Size Quilt 23 x 28 blocks

STEP H: QUILT FINISHING

Layer, baste, quilt, square, bind and label as desired.

Appendix

TABLE 1: SIMPLE/STANDARD LEAVES

Size of template (inches)	To cut leaf size (inches)	Cut width of strip from selvedge to selvedge (inches)	Number of leaves in one 40" strip	Number of standard leaves from quarter yard
Petite 2.5	2½ × 1	1¼	16	155
Norme 3	3 × 1⅛	1¼	13	122
Grande 4	4 × 1⅞	1¼	10	55
Petite 5	5 × 1¾	2	8	38
Norme 6	6 × 2⅛	2½	6	29
Grande 8	8 × 2¾	3	5	14

Use this chart as a guide for how much fabric to purchase for a project. It shows how many standard leaf shapes you can cut from strip of fabric and from a quarter yard of fabric. In general, you will get a few more leaves from a standard quarter than a fat quarter.

TABLE 2: "S" OR "Z" CURVES

Size of template (inches)	Length x Width at widest part of curve (inches): letter at intersection	Cut width of strip from selvedge to selvedge (inches)	Number of leaves in one 40" strip	Number of "S" or "Z" curves from quarter yard
Petite 2.5	5 × 1¼: e	1¾	8	84
Norme 3	6 × 1⅜: e	2	6	46
Grande 4	8 × 1⅞: e	3	5	34
Petite 5	10 × 1¾: g	2¾	4	30
Norme 6	12 × 2⅛: g	3¼	3	19
Grande 8	16 × 2⅜: g	4½	2	16

Use this chart as a guide for how much fabric to purchase for a project. It shows how many "S" or "Z" curves you can cut from a strip of fabric and from a quarter yard of fabric. In general, you will get a few more leaves from a standard quarter than a fat quarter.

TABLE 3: LEMON-SHAPED LEAVES

Size of template (inches)	Length x Width at widest part of leaf (inches)	Cut width of strip from selvedge to selvedge (inches)	Number of leaves in one 40" strip	Number of Lemon-Shaped Leaves from ½ yard of fabric
Petite 2.5	5 x 2	2¼	8	118
Norme 3	6 x 2¼	2½	6	98
Grande 4	8 x 3⅞	4	5	40
Petite 5	10 x 3½	3¾	4	31
Norme 6	12 x 4¼	4½	3	22
Grande 8	16 x 5½	5¾	2	10

Use this chart as a guide for how much fabric to purchase for a project. It shows how many lemon-shaped leaves you can cut from a ½ yard of fabric. *Technically, the leaf length is two times the curve length. However the points become so thin, they are only threads and do not hold together well. I trim approx ¼" off from each end to make a leaf ½" shorter than the original cut length. This gives room to complete your decorative stitching on the points. If you are going to top stitch without decorative stitching, you do not need to cut the points.

TABLE 4: VINE SEGMENTS

Size of template (inches)	Width and length of vine (inches)	Number of ½" x WOF vine segments from ⅛ yd.
Petite 2.5	½ x 15	7
Norme 3	½ x 18	6
Grande 4	½ x 24	5
Petite 5	½ x 15	5
Norme 6	½ x 18	4
Grande 8	½ x 24	3

TABLE 5: DIAGONAL MEASUREMENTS

Size of template (inches)	Size of the finished square with leaf placed on the diagonal (inches)	Actual diagonal measurement* (inches)	Size of cut square including seam allowance (inches)
Petite 2.5	$1\frac{7}{8}$ = 1.875	2.65	$2\frac{3}{8}$
Norme 3	$2\frac{1}{8}$ = 2.125	3.01	$2\frac{5}{8}$
Grande 4	$2\frac{7}{8}$ = 2.875	4.07	$3\frac{3}{8}$
Petite 5	$3\frac{5}{8}$ = 3.625	5.13	$4\frac{1}{8}$
Norme 6	$4\frac{1}{4}$ = 4.25	6.01	$4\frac{3}{4}$
Grande 8	$5\frac{3}{4}$ = 5.75	8.13	$6\frac{1}{4}$

*Note that the actual diagonal measurement of the finished square is slightly larger than the size of the leaf. Center the leaf on the cut square, making sure to keep a ¼" seam allowance around all four edges of square. This slight amount of play allows you to finish the edges of your appliqué prior to piecing, without your decorative stitch getting lost in the seam allowance between squares. See "Mint Chocolate" (p. 78) where a 4" leaf is placed on the diagonal of $3\frac{3}{8}$" cut squares.

TABLE 6: IDEAL TULIP COMBINATIONS

Template used to make "S" and "Z" (inches)	Standard leaf center (inches)	Finished height of tulip (inches)	"S" and "Z" shaped leaves and stems (inches)
Petite 2.5	Grande 4	4	Petite 5
Norme 3	Petite 5	5	Norme 6
Grande 4	Norme 6	6	Grande 8

TABLE 7: STANDARD QUILT SIZES IN INCHES

	Mattress top	Comforter	Bedspread	Standard batting size
Crib	28 × 52	36 × 54	DNE	45 × 60
Twin	39 × 75	65 × 88	81 × 107	72 × 90
XL Twin	39 × 80	65 × 93	81 × 112	DNE
Double/Full	54 × 75	80 × 88	96 × 107	81 × 96
XL Double/Full	54 × 80	80 × 93	96 × 112	DNE
Queen	60 × 80	86 × 93	102 × 112	90 × 108
King	78 × 80	104 × 9	120 × 112	120 × 120
Standard Pillow Case: 21 × 32		Queen Pillow Case: 21 × 36		King Pillow Case: 21 × 42

TABLE 8: TEMPLATE MULTIPLES

Multiple	Petite	Norme	Grande	Petite	Norme	Grande
1	2.5	3	4	5	6	8
2	5.0	6	8	10	12	16
3	7.5	9	12	15	18	24
4	10.0	12	16	20	24	32
5	12.5	15	20	25	30	40
6	15.0	18	24	30	36	48
7	17.5	21	28	35	42	56
8	20.0	24	32	40	48	64
9	22.5	27	36	45	54	72
10	25.0	30	40	50	60	80
11	27.5	33	44	55	66	88
12	30.0	36	48	60	72	96
13	32.5	39	52	65	78	104
14	35.0	42	56	70	84	112
15	37.5	45	60	75	90	120

TABLE EIGHT CONTINUED ON NEXT PAGE

TABLE 8: CONTINUED

Multiple	Petite	Norme	Grande	Petite	Norme	Grande
16	40.0	48	64	80	96	
17	42.5	51	68	85	102	
18	45.0	54	72	90	108	
19	47.5	57	76	95	114	
20	50.0	60	80	100	120	
21	52.5	63	84	105		
22	55.0	66	88	110		
23	57.5	69	92	115		
24	60.0	72	96	120		
25	62.5	75	100			
26	65.0	78	104			
27	67.5	81	108			

TABLE 9: SERPENTINE EDGE QUILTS AND VINES

Border Length* (inches)	2.5"	3"	4"	5"	6"	8"
8	S 1/3	R 2/3				Exact (1)
9	S 3/3	Exact (3)				
10	R 5/5	S 2/3				
11	R 3/5		R 2/3			
12	R 1/5		Exact (3)			
13	S 1/5	R 4/5	S 2/3			
14	S 3/5	R 2/5		R 2/3		
15	S 5/5 or R 5/7	Exact (5)		Exact (3)		

*Make sure your edge measurement is where you want the serpentine edge or vine to be centered. This is not the edge of the quilt. Must be at least 1½" in from each edge.

**Stretch (S) or Reduce (R) the number of curves indicated on chart by one half inch.
For example, S 1/3 means mark three curves, but stretch one of these three curves by ½".
R 2/7 means reduce mark seven curves, but reduce the size of two of those curves by ½" each.
Exact (3) means three curves will fit exactly.

TABLE 9 CONTINUED ON NEXT PAGE

Border Length* (inches)	2.5"	3"	4"	5"	6"	8"
16	R 3/7	S 2/5		S 2/3		
17	R 1/7	S 4/5			R 2/3	
18	S 1/7	R 6/7	R 4/5		Exact (3)	
19	S 3/7	R 4/7	R 2/5		S 2/3	
20	S 5/7 or R 5/9	R 2/7	Exact (5)			
21	R 3/9	Exact (7)	S 2/5			
22	R 1/9	S 2/7	S 4/5			
23	S 1/9	S 4/7		R 4/5		R 2/3
24	S 3/9	S 6/7 or R 6/9		R 2/5		Exact (3)
25	S 5/9 or R 5/11	R 4/9	R 6/7	Exact (5)		S 2/3
26	R 3/11	R 2/9	R 4/7	S 2/5		
27	R 1/11	Exact (9)	R 2/7	S 4/5		
28	S 1/11	S 2/9	Exact (7)		R 4/5	
29	S 3/11	S 4/9	S 2/7		R 2/5	
30	S 5/11 or R 5/13	S 6/9 or R 6/11	S 4/7		Exact (5)	
31	R 3/13	R 4/11	S 6/7		S 2/5	
32	R 1/13	R 2/11	R 8/9	R 6/7	S 4/5	
33	S 1/13	Exact (11)	R 6/9	R 4/7		
34	S 3/13	S 2/11	R 4/9	R 2/7		
35	S 5/13 or R 5/15	S 4/11	R 2/9	Exact (7)		
36	R 3/15	S 6/9 or R 6/13	Exact (9)	S 2/7		
37	R 1/15	R 4/13	S 2/9	S 4/7		
38	S 1/15	R 2/13	S 4/9	S 6/7		R 4/5
39	S 3/15	Exact (13)	S 6/9		R 6/7	R 2/5
40	S 5/13 or R 5/17	S 2/13	S 8/9 or R 8/11		R 4/7	Exact (5)
41	R 3/17	S 4/13	R 6/11	R 8/9	R 2/7	S 2/5
42	R 1/17	S 6/13 or R 6/15	R 4/11	R 6/9	Exact (7)	S 4/5

TABLE 9 CONTINUED ON NEXT PAGE

Border Length* (inches)	2.5"	3"	4"	5"	6"	8"
43	S 1/17	R 4/15	R 2/11	R 4/9	S 2/7	
44	S 3/17	R 2/15	Exact (11)	R 2/9	S 4/7	
45	S 5/17 or R 5/19	Exact (15)	S 2/11	Exact (9)	S 6/7	
46	R 3/19	S 2/15	S 4/11	S 2/9		
47	R 1/19	S 4/15	S 6/11	S 4/9		
48	S 1/19	S 6/15 or R 6/17	S 8/11 or R 8/13	S 6/9		
49	S 3/19	R 4/17	R 6/13	S 8/9		
50	S 5/19 or R 5/21	R 2/17	R 4/13	R 10/11	R 8/9	
51	R 3/21	Exact (17)	R 2/13	R 8/11	R 6/9	
52	R 1/21	S 2/17	Exact (13)	R 6/11	R 4/9	
53	S 1/21	S 4/17	S 2/13	R 4/11	R 2/9	R 6/7
54	S 3/21	S 6/17 or R 6/19	S 4/13	R 2/11	Exact (9)	R 4/7
55	S 5/21 or R 5/23	R 4/19	S 6/13	Exact (11)	S 2/9	R 2/7
56	R 3/23	R 2/19	S 8/13 or R 8/15	S 2/11	S 4/9	Exact (7)
57	R 1/23	Exact (19)	R 6/15	S 4/11	S 6/9	S 2/7
58	S 1/23	S 2/19	R 4/15	S 6/11	S 8/9	S 4/7
59	S 3/23	S 4/19	R 2/15	S 8/11		S 6/7
60	S 5/23 or R 5/25	S 6/19 or R 6/21	Exact (15)	S 10/11 or R 10/13		
61	R 3/25	R 4/21	S 2/15	R 8/13	R 10/11	
62	R 1/25	R 2/21	S 4/15	R 6/13	R 8/11	
63	S 1/25	Exact (21)	S 6/15	R 4/13	R 6/11	
64	S 3/25	S 2/21	S 8/15 or R 8/17	R 2/13	R 4/11	
65	S 5/25 or R 5/27	S 4/21	R 6/17	Exact (13)	R 2/11	
66	R 3/27	S 6/21 or R 6/23	R 4/17	S 2/13	Exact (11)	
67	R 1/27	R 4/23	R 2/17	S 4/13	S 2/11	
68	S 1/27	R 2/23	Exact (17)	S 6/13	S 4/11	R 8/9

TABLE 9 CONTINUED ON NEXT PAGE

Border Length* (inches)	2.5"	3"	4"	5"	6"	8"
69	S 3/27	Exact (23)	S 2/17	S 8/13	S 6/11	R 6/9
70	S 5/27 or R 5/29	S 2/23	S 4/17	S 10/13 or R 10/15	S 8/11	R 4/9
71	R 3/29	S 4/23	S 6/17	R 8/15	S 10/11	R 2/9
72	R 1/29	S 6/23 or R 6/25	S 8/17 or R 8/19	R 6/15	R 12/13	Exact (9)
73	S 1/29	R 4/25	R 6/19	R 4/15	R 10/13	S 2/9
74	S 3/29	R 2/25	R 4/19	R 2/15	R 8/13	S 4/9
75	S 5/29 or R 5/31	Exact (25)	R 2/19	Exact (15)	R 6/13	S 6/9
76	R 3/31	S 2/25	Exact (19)	S 2/15	R 4/13	S 8/9
77	R 1/31	S 4/25	S 2/19	S 4/15	R 2/13	
78	S 1/31	S 6/25 or R 6/27	S 4/19	S 6/15	Exact (13)	
79	S 3/31	R 4/27	S 6/19	S 8/15	S 2/13	
80	S 5/31 or R 5/33	R 2/27	S 8/19 or R 8/21	S 10/15 or R 10/17	S 4/13	
81	R 3/33	Exact (27)	R 6/21	R 8/17	S 6/13	
82	R 1/33	S 2/27	R 4/21	R 6/17	S 8/13	
83	S 1/33	S 4/27	R 2/21	R 4/17	S 10/13	R 10/11
84	S 3/33	S 6/27 or R 6/29	Exact (21)	R 2/17	S 12/13 or R 12/15	R 8/11
85	S 5/33 or R 5/35	R 4/29	S 2/21	Exact (17)	R 10/15	R 6/11
86	R 3/35	R 2/29	S 4/21	S 2/17	R 8/15	R 4/11
87	R 1/35	Exact (29)	S 6/21	S 4/17	R 6/15	R 2/11
88	S 1/35	S 2/29	S 8/21 or R 8/23	S 6/17	R 4/15	Exact (11)
89	S 3/35	S 4/29	R 6/23	S 8/17	R 2/15	S 2/11
90	S 5/35or R 5/37	S 6/29 or R 6/31	R 4/23	S 10/17 or R 10/19	Exact (15)	S 4/11
91	R 3/37	R 4/31	R 2/23	R 8/19	S 2/15	S 6/11
92	R 1/37	R 2/31	Exact (23)	R 6/19	S 4/15	S 8/11
93	S 1/37	Exact (31)	S 2/23	R 4/19	S 6/15	S 10/11
94	S 3/37	S 2/31	S 4/23	R 2/19	S 8/15	

TABLE 9 CONTINUED ON NEXT PAGE

Border Length[*] (inches)	2.5"	3"	4"	5"	6"	8"
95	S 5/37 or R 5/39	S 4/31	S 6/23	Exact (19)	S 10/15	
96	R 3/39	S 6/31 or R 6/33	S 8/23 or R 8/25	S 2/19	S 12/15 or R 12/17	
97	R 1/39	R 4/33	R 6/25	S 4/19	R 10/17	
98	S 1/39	R 2/33	R 4/25	S 6/19	R 8/17	R 12/13
99	S 3/39	Exact (33)	R 2/25	S 8/19	R 6/17	R 10/13
100	S 5/39 or R 5/41	S 2/33	Exact (25)	S 10/19 or R 10/21	R 4/17	R 8/13
101	R 3/41	S 4/33	S 2/25	R 8/21	R 2/17	R 6/13
102	R 1/41	S 6/33 or R 6/35	S 4/25	R 6/21	Exact (17)	R 4/13
103	S 1/41	R 4/35	S 6/25	R 4/21	S 2/17	R 2/13
104	S 3/41	R 2/35	S 8/25 or R 8/27	R 2/21	S 4/17	Exact (13)
105	S 5/51or R 5/43	Exact (35)	R 6/27	Exact (21)	S 6/17	S 2/13
106	R 3/43	S 2/35	R 4/27	S 2/21	S 8/17	S 4/13
107	R 1/43	S 4/35	R 2/27	S 4/21	S 10/17	S 6/13
108	S 1/43	S 6/35 or R 6/37	Exact (27)	S 6/21	S 12/17 or R 12/19	S 8/13
109	S 3/43	R 4/37	S 2/27	S 8/21	R 10/19	S 10/13
110	S 5/43 or R 5/45	R 2/37	S 4/27	S 10/21 or R 10/23	R 8/19	S 12/13
111	R 3/45	Exact (37)	S 6/27	R 8/23	R 6/19	
112	R 1/45	S 2/37	S 8/27 or R 8/29	R 6/23	R 4/19	
113	S 1/45	S 4/37	R 6/29	R 4/23	R 2/19	
114	S 3/45	S 6/37 or R 6/39	R 4/29	R 2/23	Exact (19)	R 12/15
115	S 5/45 or R 5/47	R 4/39	R 2/29	Exact (23)	S 2/19	R 10/15
116	R 3/47	R 2/39	Exact (29)	S 2/23	S 4/19	R 8/15
117	R 1/47	Exact (39)	S 2/29	S 4/23	S 6/19	R 6/15
118	S 1/47	S 2/39	S 4/29	S 6/23	S 8/19	R 4/15
119	S 3/47	S 4/39	S 6/29	S 8/23	S 10/19	R 2/15

TABLE 9 CONTINUED ON NEXT PAGE

TABLE 9: CONTINUED

Border Length* (inches)	2.5"	3"	4"	5"	6"	8"
120	S 5/47 or R 5/49	S 6/39 or R 6/41	S 8/29 or R 8/31	S 10/23 or R 10/25	S 12/19 or R 12/21	Exact (15)
121	R 3/49	R 4/41	R 6/31	R 8/25	R 10/21	S 2/15
122	R 1/49	R 2/41	R 4/31	R 6/25	R 8/21	S 4/15

TABLE 10: SCALLOPED EDGE QUILTS

Border Length* (inches)	2.5"	3"	4"	5"	6"	8"
8	S 1/3	R 2/3	Exact (2)			Exact (1)
9	S 3/3 or R 2/4	Exact (3)	S 2/2			
10	Exact (4)	S 2/3				
11	S 2/4	R 2/4	R 2/3		R 2/2	
12	R 1/5	Exact (4)	Exact (3)		Exact (2)	
13	S 1/5	S 2/4	S 2/3		S 2/2	
14	S 3/5 or R 2/6	R 2/5		R 2/3		
15	Exact (6)	Exact (5)	R 2/4	Exact (3)		R 2/2
16	S 2/6	S 2/5	Exact (4)	S 2/3		Exact (2)
17	R 1/7	R 2/6	S 2/4		R 2/3	S 2/2
18	S 1/7	Exact (6)	R 4/5	R 4/4	Exact (3)	
19	S 3/7 or R 2/8	S 2/6	R 2/5	R 2/4	S 2/3	
20	Exact (8)	R 2/7	Exact (5)	Exact (4)		
21	S 2/8	Exact (7)	S 2/5	S 2/4		
22	R 1/9	S 2/7	S 4/5 or R 4/6	S 4/4	R 4/4	
23	S 1/9	R 2/8	R 2/6	R 4/5	R 2/4	R 2/3
24	S 3/9 or R 2/10	Exact (8)	Exact (6)	R 2/5	Exact (4)	Exact (3)
25	Exact (10)	S 2/8	S 2/6	Exact (5)	S 2/4	S 2/3

*Make sure your edge measurement is where you want the scalloped edge or vine to be centered. This is not the edge of the quilt. Must be at least 1½" in from each edge.

**Stretch (S) or Reduce (R) the number of curves indicated on chart by one half inch.

TABLE 10 CONTINUED ON NEXT PAGE

Border Length* (inches)	2.5"	3"	4"	5"	6"	8"
26	S 2/10	R 2/9	S 4/6 or R 4/7	S 2/5	S 4/4	
27	R 1/11	Exact (9)	R 2/7	S 4/5		
28	S 1/11	S 2/9	Exact (7)	R 4/6	R 4/5	
29	S 3/11 or R 2/12	R 2/10	S 2/7	R 2/6	R 2/5	
30	Exact (12)	Exact (10)	S 4/7 or R 4/8	Exact (6)	Exact (5)	R 4/4
31	S 2/12	S 2/10	R 2/8	S 2/6	S 2/5	R 2/4
32	R 1/13	R 2/11	Exact (8)	S 4/6	S 4/5	Exact (4)
33	S 1/13	Exact (11)	S 2/8	R 4/7		S 2/4
34	S 3/13 or R 2/14	S 2/11	S 4/8 or R 4/9	R 2/7	R 4/6	S 4/4
35	Exact (14)	R 2/12	R 2/9	Exact (7)	R 2/6	
36	S 2/14	Exact (12)	Exact (9)	S 2/7	Exact (6)	
37	R 1/15	S 2/12	S 2/9	S 4/7	S 2/6	
38	S 1/15	R 2/13	S 4/9 or R 4/10	R 4/8	S 4/6	R 4/5
39	S 3/15 or R 2/16	Exact (13)	R 2/10	R 2/8	S 6/6 or R 6/7	R 2/5
40	Exact (16)	S 2/13	Exact (10)	Exact (8)	R 4/7	Exact (5)
41	S 2/16	R 2/14	S 2/10	S 2/8	R 2/7	S 2/5
42	R 1/17	Exact (14)	S 4/10 or R 4/11	S 4/8	Exact (7)	S 4/5
43	S 1/17	S 2/14	R 2/11	R 4/9	S 2/7	
44	S 3/17 or R 2/18	R 2/15	Exact (11)	R 2/9	S 4/7	
45	Exact (18)	Exact (15)	S 2/11	Exact (9)	S 6/7 or R 6/8	R 6/6
46	S 2/18	S 2/15	S 4/11 or R 4/12	S 2/9	R 4/8	R 4/6
47	R 1/19	R 2/16	R 2/12	S 4/9	R 2/8	R 2/6
48	S 1/19	Exact (16)	Exact (12)	R 4/10	Exact (8)	Exact (6)
49	S 3/19 or R 2/20	S 2/16	S 2/12	R 2/10	S 2/8	S 2/6
50	Exact (20)	R 2/17	S 4/12 or R 4/13	Exact (10)	S 4/8	S 4/6

TABLE 10 CONTINUED ON NEXT PAGE

Border Length* (inches)	2.5"	3"	4"	5"	6"	8"
51	S 2/20	Exact (17)	R 2/13	S 2/10	S 6/8 or R 6/9	S 6/6
52	R 1/21	S 2/17	Exact (13)	S 4/10	R 4/9	
53	S 1/21	R 2/18	S 2/13	R 4/11	R 2/9	R 6/7
54	S 3/21 or R 2/22	Exact (18)	S 4/13 or R 4/14	R 2/11	Exact (9)	R 4/7
55	Exact (22)	S 2/18	R 2/14	Exact (11)	S 2/9	R 2/7
56	S 2/22	R 2/19	Exact (14)	S 2/11	S 4/9	Exact (7)
57	R 1/23	Exact (19)	S 2/14	S 4/11	S 6/9 or R 6/10	S 2/7
58	S 1/23	S 2/19	S 4/14 or R 4/15	R 4/12	R 4/10	S 4/7
59	S 3/23 or R 2/24	R 2/20	R 2/15	R 2/12	R 2/10	S 6/7
60	Exact (24)	Exact (20)	Exact (15)	Exact (12)	Exact (10)	R 8/8
61	S 2/24	S 2/20	S 2/15	S 2/12	S 2/10	R 6/8
62	R 1/25	R 2/21	S 4/15 or R 4/16	S 4/12	S 4/10	R 4/8
63	S 1/25	Exact (21)	R 2/16	R 4/13	S 6/10 or R 6/11	R 2/8
64	S 3/25 or R 2/26	S 2/21	Exact (16)	R 2/13	R 4/11	Exact (8)
65	Exact (26)	R 2/22	S 2/16	Exact (13)	R 2/11	S 2/8
66	S 2/26	Exact (22)	S 4/16 or R 4/17	S 2/13	Exact (11)	S 4/8
67	R 1/27	S 2/22	R 2/17	S 4/13	S 2/11	S 6/8
68	S 1/27	R 2/23	Exact (17)	R 4/14	S 4/11	S 8/8 or R 8/9
69	S 3/27 or R 2/28	Exact (23)	S 2/17	R 2/14	S 6/11 or R 6/12	R 6/9
70	Exact (28)	S 2/23	S 4/17 or R 4/18	Exact (14)	R 4/12	R 4/9
71	S 2/28	R 2/24	R 2/18	S 2/14	R 2/12	R 2/9
72	R 1/29	Exact (24)	Exact (18)	S 4/14	Exact (12)	Exact (9)
73	S 1/29	S 2/24	S 2/18	R 4/15	S 2/12	S 2/9
74	S 3/29 or R 2/30	R 2/25	S 4/18 or R 4/19	R 2/15	S 4/12	S 4/9

TABLE 10 CONTINUED ON NEXT PAGE

Border Length* (inches)	2.5"	3"	4"	5"	6"	8"
75	Exact (30)	Exact (25)	R 2/19	Exact (15)	S 6/12 or R 6/13	S 6/9
76	S 2/30	S 2/25	Exact (19)	S 2/15	R 4/13	S 8/9 or R 8/10
77	R 1/31	R 2/26	S 2/19	S 4/15	R 2/13	R 6/10
78	S 1/31	Exact (26)	S 4/19 or R 4/20	R 4/16	Exact (13)	R 4/10
79	S 3/31 or R 2/32	S 2/26	R 2/20	R 2/16	S 2/13	R 2/10
80	Exact (32)	R 2/27	Exact (20)	Exact (16)	S 4/13	Exact (10)
81	S 2/32	Exact (27)	S 2/20	S 2/16	S 6/13 or R 6/14	S 2/10
82	R 1/33	S 2/27	S 4/20 or R 4/21	S 4/16	R 4/14	S 4/10
83	S 1/33	R 2/28	R 2/21	R 4/17	R 2/14	S 6/10
84	S 3/33 or R 2/34	Exact (28)	Exact (21)	R 2/17	Exact (14)	S 8/10 or R 8/11
85	Exact (34)	S 2/28	S 2/21	Exact (17)	S 2/14	R 6/11
86	S 2/34	R 2/29	S 4/21 or R 4/22	S 2/17	S 4/14	R 4/11
87	R 1/35	Exact (29)	R 2/22	S 4/17	S 6/14 or R 6/15	R 2/11
88	S 1/35	S 2/29	Exact (22)	R 4/18	R 4/15	Exact (11)
89	S 3/35 or R 2/36	R 2/30	S 2/22	R 2/18	R 2/15	S 2/11
90	Exact (36)	Exact (30)	S 4/22 or R 4/23	Exact (18)	Exact (15)	S 4/11
91	S 2/36	S 2/30	R 2/23	S 2/18	S 2/15	S 6/11
92	R 1/37	R 2/31	Exact (23)	S 4/18	S 4/15	S 8/11 or R 8/12
93	S 1/37	Exact (31)	S 2/23	R 4/19	S 6/15 or R 6/16	R 6/12
94	S 3/37 or R 2/38	S 2/31	S 4/23 or R 4/24	R 2/19	R 4/16	R 4/12
95	Exact (38)	R 2/32	R 2/24	Exact (19)	R 2/16	R 2/12
96	S 2/38	Exact (32)	Exact (24)	S 2/19	Exact (16)	Exact (12)
97	R 1/39	S 2/32	S 2/24	S 4/19	S 2/16	S 2/12

TABLE 10 CONTINUED ON NEXT PAGE

Border Length* (inches)	2.5"	3"	4"	5"	6"	8"
98	S 1/39	R 2/33	S 4/24 or R 4/25	R 4/20	S 4/16	S 4/12
99	S 3/39 or R 2/40	Exact (33)	R 2/25	R 2/20	S 6/16 or R 6/17	S 6/12
100	Exact (40)	S 2/33	Exact (25)	Exact (20)	R 4/17	S 8/12 or R 8/13
101	S 2/40	R 2/34	S 2/25	S 2/20	R 2/17	R 6/13
102	R 1/41	Exact (34)	S 4/25 or R 4/26	S 4/20	Exact (17)	R 4/13
103	S 1/41	S 2/34	R 2/26	R 4/21	S 2/17	R 2/13
104	S 3/41 or R 2/42	R 2/35	Exact (26)	R 2/21	S 4/17	Exact (13)
105	Exact (42)	Exact (35)	S 2/26	Exact (21)	S 6/17 or R 6/18	S 2/13
106	S 2/42	S 2/35	S 4/26 or R 4/27	S 2/21	R 4/18	S 4/13
107	R 1/43	R 2/36	R 2/27	S 4/21	R 2/18	S 6/13
108	S 1/43	Exact (36)	Exact (27)	R 4/22	Exact (18)	S 8/13 or R 8/14
109	S 3/43 or R 2/44	S 2/36	S 2/27	R 2/22	S 2/18	R 6/14
110	Exact (44)	R 2/37	S 4/27 or R 4/28	Exact (22)	S 4/18	R 4/14
111	S 2/44	Exact (37)	R 2/27	S 2/22	S 6/18 or R 6/19	R 2/14
112	R 1/45	S 2/37	Exact (28)	S 4/22	R 4/19	Exact (14)
113	S 1/45	R 2/38	S 2/28	R 4/23	R 2/19	S 2/14
114	S 3/45 or R 2/46	Exact (38)	S 4/28 or R 4/29	R 2/23	Exact (19)	S 4/14
115	Exact (46)	S 2/38	R 2/29	Exact (23)	S 2/19	S 6/14
116	S 2/46	R 2/39	Exact (29)	S 2/23	S 4/19	S 8/14 or R 8/15
117	R 1/47	Exact (39)	S 2/29	S 4/23	S 6/19 or R 6/20	R 6/15
118	S 1/47	S 2/39	S 4/29 or R 4/30	R 4/24	R 4/20	R 4/15
119	S 3/47 or R 2/48	R 2/40	R 2/30	R 2/24	R 2/20	R 2/15

TABLE 10 CONTINUED ON NEXT PAGE

TABLE 10: CONTINUED

Border Length* (inches)	2.5"	3"	4"	5"	6"	8"
120	Exact (48)	Exact (40)	Exact (30)	Exact (24)	Exact (20)	Exact (15)
121	S 2/48	S 2/40	S 2/30	S 2/24	S 2/20	S 2/15
122	R 1/49	R 2/41	S 4/30 or R 4/31	S 4/24	S 4/20	S 4/15

QUILTING DESIGNS

Feather Quilting

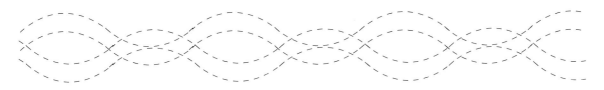

Border Chain with ½" spacing

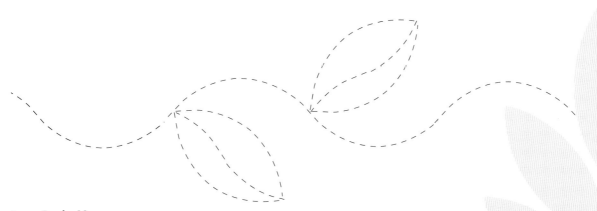

Large Border Vine

Border Chain with ¼" spacing

Small Border Vine

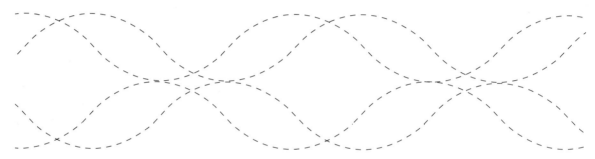

Off-Set Double Lemon-Shaped Leaves

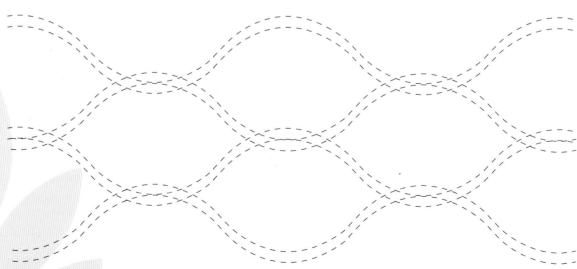

Interlocking Lemon Shapes with ¼" spacing